THE
MIND
IS THE
MAP

Christina Reeves

Dimitrios Spanos

THE
MIND
IS THE
MAP

*Awareness is the Compass, and Emotional Intelligence
is the Key to Living Mindfully from the Heart*

The Mind is the Map

By Dimitrios Spanos and Christina Reeves

1. <PSYCHOLOGY / Emotions> 2. <BODY, MIND & SPIRIT / Inspiration & Personal Growth> 3. <SELF-HELP / Personal Growth / Success >

Hardback ISBN: 978-1-7322054-0-6

Paperback ISBN: 978-1-7322054-2-0

Workbook ISBN: 978-1-7322054-4-4

eBook: 978-1-7322054-1-3

Audio ISBN: 978-1-7322054-3-7

Library of Congress Control Number: 2018909359

Cover design by https://damonza.com

Edited by: Diana Ennen - https://virtualwordpublishing.com

Printed in the United States of America

Publisher: Eudaimonia Center LLC

      23-31 37th Street, Astoria, N.Y 11105

      718-397-0290

https://themindisthemap.com

TABLE OF CONTENTS

ACKNOWLEDGEMENTS

During the process of writing this book, we were both empowered by recollections of our own evolution. As we continued our journey of awakening and growth, new understandings found their way into our work. Others that we have worked with often stimulated those understandings, giving inspiration to us and to one another in the sharing of their struggles and victories. We thank each and every one of them.

Many family members and friends have been with us throughout this project in the way of encouragement and support, and we thank them especially for their tolerance enduring our sometimes long and seemingly endless conversations about how the book was coming along. It is great to have you with us on our journey.

Many others have helped in the production of this book, either personally or professionally, and a very special thanks to our team. Thanks to Terry Green for your thorough and professional administrative support on the project, and for assisting us in selecting our team members as well as your warm, caring interaction with all of us. Much gratitude goes out to Diana Ennen for setting the processes into action and for being its caring shepherd from the edit to print and beyond into the marketing strategies. We thank you Diana for your unfailing support. Your enthusiasm has been a guiding light and your touch present in every aspect of the project. Gabriela, thank you for your graphic designs created from our patchwork scribbles. It was such a blessing to have you on the team. Cheryl, thank you for your contribution, your savvy wisdom, and your assistance in uploading the book on the various distribution platforms was invaluable. You made it possible to enjoy an experience that might otherwise have been a stressful one. Thank you Deborah for your expert assistance with setting up the social media platforms.

Thanks to the amazing team at Damonza. For the book cover design, we thank Benjamin and Chrissy; and for the interior formatting of the book, once again, well done Chrissy. Benjamin, you did amazing work on the book trailer—you told our entire story in less than four minutes, and you did it well. Thank you so very much.

Special thanks go to Zach Parker, for your expert design and setup of our book's landing page, providing us with an invaluable forum for interaction with our readers. Your keen understanding of our work added substantially to the process and your precious presence added to our stimulating zoom meetings…smiling.

Big thanks to Julie and to Christine from our office for the research and administrative work done behind the scenes that made our workload so much easier.

To all the teachers, scientists, and philosophers who have shared their wisdom with us and for all those who showed up easily in our lives exactly when we needed them creating even more opportunities for us to grow and enabling us to be able to serve others, we are sincerely grateful.

Finally, to our beloved Muse, we thank you for the spark of light that brought us together for this collaborative effort, for igniting our passion, and for gifting us with inspiration to write this book. Through this writing, we became more conscious of the living aspect of Athena, as she helps us develop a greater imagination of the real world and experience the power of Universal Energy and love. Athena is part of Sophia, the Soul of the world. Connecting with her wisdom develops a powerful mind. To the small voice within we are eternally grateful.

DEDICATIONS

*This book is dedicated to my lovely wife, Maria,
my two wonderful children, Marianna and
Stephanos, my son-in-law, Fahmi, and my adorable
Mom. All of them have contributed so much
towards shaping my own Map of the Mind.*

Love and Light - Dimitrios

*And to my beautiful illuminated daughter, Julie,
who introduced me to the path of light with the
miracle of her birth. I'm so grateful. Her presence
in my life has continuously awakened the light
and love within me. To my wonderful son-in-law,
Darwin, and my beloved grandchildren, Katelyn
and Tristan, may they always be blessed living
the presence of love and light from the heart.*

Much love, Christina (Marmie)

"One looks back with appreciation to the brilliant teachers, but with gratitude to those who touched our human feelings. The curriculum is so much necessary raw material, but warmth is the vital element for the growing plant and for the soul of the child."

- Carl Jung

FOREWORD BY DIMITRIOS SPANOS AND CHRISTINA REEVES

In a dialog format we offer our many years of experience in the field of human potential with ideas and insights into how you can expand your Awareness to become more conscious using two systems we have created—*The Mind is the Map* and what we call the "*Writing on Our Walls.*" We will guide you toward your personal self-discovery process and explain how these discoveries affect your life experiences. You will learn to use new tools that can empower you to lead fulfilling personal and professional lives.

We have both been blessed with many talented teachers over the years and a host of experiences that contributed to the knowledge and wisdom for developing these processes and writing this book. The processes have been presented to many others over the last decade, including individuals, life coaches, psychologists and psychotherapists, doctors, sociologists, health and wellness professionals, and in general anyone working on their own spiritual path or wanting to understand and improve their life experiences. The book has been written in order by the processes and we recommend you read it in the order it has been presented. There is a self-help section at the end of each chapter for "Making it Personal." We encourage you to spend time reflecting with these sections.

As we escort you through this unique experience, you will come to understand why *The Mind is the Map* and how *The Writing on Our*

Walls actually echoes into your world creating your current reality. You will have many opportunities to examine the various areas of your life, from work and career, to your relationships with yourself and others. As you progress through the chapters, you will learn more about yourself and you will have many opportunities to learn how to work with your own experiences, your relationships with others, your emotions, and your behavioral patterns.

We will help you to understand your often-hidden belief systems and how they came to be *written on your walls*. You will learn how this writing affects your choices and your experiences, causing you to repeat the same patterns in your life, over and over again. This is a natural progressive function of this book and will serve to launch you beyond your "limits" and free any limitations for you. In the process you will, of course, realize that there is nothing more important or more exciting than turning possibilities and opportunities into personal realities as you learn how to live your life with *Emotional Intelligence* and see how *YOU can be a long-term advisor to yourself*.

Expect and allow miracles and synchronicity to show up in the most amazing ways and you will undoubtedly experience a few "ah-ha" moments, and in the most intelligent way, you will realize that you are one with all that is.

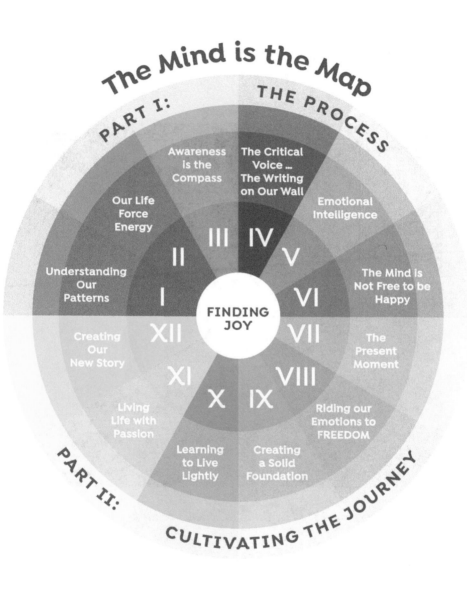

The Mind is the Map

PART I: THE PROCESS

Awareness is the Compass

The Critical Voice ... The Writing on Our Wall

Our Life Force Energy

Emotional Intelligence

III IV V

Understanding Our Patterns

II

The Mind is Not Free to be Happy

I VI

Creating Our New Story

XII FINDING JOY VII

The Present Moment

XI VIII

Living Life with Passion

X IX

Riding our Emotions to FREEDOM

Learning to Live Lightly

Creating a Solid Foundation

PART II: CULTIVATING THE JOURNEY

"Who looks outside dreams? Who looks inside awakens."

- Carl Jung

PROLOGUE BY CHRISTINA REEVES

We all know what it's like to be triggered—to have said something we wish we hadn't or to have reacted in a way that wasn't helpful. What if there was a way to interrupt our knee-jerk responses and make different choices? Each of us gets hooked in habitual ways of seeing the world, but how we respond to these situations will in a large part determine how much peace and freedom we experience in our lives.

The purpose of this book is to help you see the ways in which you get caught or "hooked" in habitual responses to life, and how you can learn to choose a "fresh alternative." This then allows you to experience a life of freedom, joy, and true happiness. Within the pages of this book, Dimitrios and I share the liberating wisdom of an approach that we both use in our personal daily practices, along with tools for putting it to work in your own lives.

Following is an excerpt from my personal journal, one that started me on my personal path to Self-Discovery:

"Change entered my life suddenly and painfully, causing huge shifts in my internal and external world. While I did not understand it at the time, later, upon reflection, I was guided to see things about myself, my relationships, and my life. I was resistant, of course, and the more resistant I was to change, the bigger the messages and the deeper the hole I was falling into became.

It arrived with a huge announcement and momentous shift in every aspect of my life. In some extraordinary way, it seemingly happened without the usual pattern of my efforts to control my life. I was feeling an urgent desire to explore, discover, and take action to overhaul my life. It was during my own process of discovery that there were times I found that change had happened, seemingly without my involvement. I even wondered whether all of my hard work had anything to do with it or if it just happened by way of grace.

This doesn't mean that my efforts played no part in the miracle of change—it did. It's just that looking back on it now I see that my efforts were only part of the picture that finally revealed itself to me in the form of shifting my thoughts and my life patterns. Through my new understanding of the workings of the mind, a softening occurred that led me to living from my heart.

I came to understand that the same laws that govern everything in our Universe were overseeing my own internal and external changes. I lived in the realm of my busyness, believing that everything external in my life was the reflection of who I was, which was what I had come to call "*my winning formula.*"

Sometimes the hard part is to accept life as it happens and to stop and let go of our need to control life and hand it over to the Universe. For me, this happened by way of distraction and disruption. My attention was being called away to other more pressing concerns related to mere survival, or so I thought. I was losing everything I considered important in my life. At that time, I was not "*seeing*" the silence of a Divine embrace and that the miracle of change was happening.

My first visit to my own coach and mentor was not what I

expected. Somehow, I believe this might be true for others who experience their first "*therapy*" session as well. She began by asking me to tell her something about myself. So naturally, I told her all about what I do, what I have done, accomplished, acquired, etc.

She sat there looking at me and after what seemed like a very long time, she said very softly, "Thanks for sharing your stories, Christina. But what I really want to know is more about you."

Now it was my silence that seemed to pierce the space between us. The volume of my mind chatter was soaring rapidly saying things like, "What does she mean? I just told her about me. These aren't stories. This is who I am." I finally replied, "I'm not sure what you mean. I've just told you about myself."

Again, with this gentle voice as if I was fragile or something, she said, "Why don't you begin by telling me what you are feeling right now?" I answered with, "Well, they said I am a workaholic and I leave no room in my life for anything else."

"Yes, I understand that is why you came to see me. How do you feel?"

"You mean about what they said?"

"No, Christina. It's not about what they said. What I want to know is how you are feeling. How do you feel about you, about your life, and about life itself?"

The mind chatter was kicking in again. Why was she speaking to me as if I were broken or something? "Well, I don't know. I never really thought about it."

She put down her notepad and reached over to take my hand. "Feeling is not really a thinking exercise, Christina. Why not try to let go of your mind and simply tell me how you feel."

Now I did feel fragile! Wow, how did she do that? I was feeling great, but now I'm thinking, "What if I was broken?" There was another seemingly long silence and when I finally did speak, I could hardly hear or recognize myself. "I don't know how I feel. I really don't feel very much at all." What I meant to say was, "I have lots of feelings about things and I feel for others, but when it comes to my feelings, I don't know how I feel." With the words having just tumbled out from my now quivering lips, I was stunned and thought, *"Who was that speaking? Did I really just say that?"*

"Well Christina, that's a very good place for us to begin our process of discovery. I'll see you again next week and we'll pick it up from there."

Exiting her office, my mind chatter increased another tenfold. Discovery? What is that? And what is it we're looking for? And what's up with that unknown awkward voice within me that stumbled and tripped on the words that came spilling out along with my tears. I became concerned.

Back in my car, I actually shouted out loud to no one in particular and said, "Who was that voice?" Although I was laughing at myself, on some other level I felt fear in the pit of my stomach. Then I stopped laughing as a powerful thought occurred to me and the mind chatter stopped. I thought, "What if someone within us is listening?" Little did I know that I had reached a choice point in my life and I was about to embark on a very long and equally rewarding journey.

...end of journal...

How many of you wonder why we do what we do and why we keep doing that? Does this sound familiar? "No matter what I do, the results are always the same." Do you ever wonder, "What is wrong with me? Why do I keep doing the same things again and again, even when I know better? Why does he/she always seem to do that?" Or even, "Where did my child pick up that behavior?"

Let's begin our journey of "*The Mind is the Map*" by looking at our perspectives. It is important to understand that what you see is not in the data. It is determined by our own perceptions or our interpretation of the data. Perception is our belief. When we truly believe in a perception, we see it as the one and only reality, ignoring all other possibilities. Our mind has a host of programmed perceptions that directly shape the biology, behavior, and character of our lives. Therefore, it is important that we know the origin of these perceptions.

As Aristotle puts it, *"The mind is nothing before it thinks."* In responding to the interaction problem, he claims, "Have not we already disposed of the difficulty about interaction involving a common element, when we said that mind is in a sense potentially whatever is thinkable, though actually it is nothing until it has thought? What it thinks must be in it just as characters may be said to be on a writing tablet on which as yet nothing actually stands written: this is exactly what happens with the mind."

English Philosopher, John Locke, supports this blank slate theory, stating that, "People learn and acquire ideas from external forces or the environment. Humans are born with an empty mind, having no knowledge whatsoever. People acquire ideas from the surrounding world, turning simple ideas into complex ones." This blank slate of the mind starts off devoid of any knowledge, but then it is *"written on"* as a person lives and experiences.

We have no individual personality or identity until after we are born. There is no built-in mental content. It is the environment that has the ability to shape our individual mind and experiences. Each new experience serves as a stage of growth, expanding possibilities and gathering new knowledge—forming our human traits, personality, and character of who we think we are. Our identity is defined entirely by our experiences and sensory perceptions of the outside world.

Generally, people now recognize the fact that most of the brain is indeed pre-programmed and organized in order to process sensory input, motor control, emotions, and natural responses. These pre-programmed parts of the brain then learn and refine their ability to perform their tasks. The only true clean slate in the brain is the neo-cortex. This part of the brain is involved in thought and decision-making and is strongly linked with the amygdala. The amygdala is involved in responses such as fight or flight and emotions, and like other parts of the brain, it is largely "pre-programmed." But it has space to learn within its *"programming."* There are three ways the subconscious is programmed. These include:

1. Innate Vital Functions: These are the natural functions of new life. We are born to survive in our world. We are born knowing how to breathe, how to suckle, how to swallow, how to eliminate waste, and so forth. We are born with an innate immune system as our first line of defense. In fact, our physical bodies *"operating systems"* are fully functional but we have no cognitive database.

2. Experiential Memories: These are our life-controlling perceptions that come from experiential memories downloaded into the subconscious mind. Examples include: If you were raised in a war-torn environment, you might have a lot of fear and trauma stored in your earliest memories. If you experienced poverty in your childhood, you might grow up with a perception that life is hard because you have early childhood memories of lack and struggle.

3. Subconscious Mind: This is the most influential perception. The programming of the subconscious mind occurs between birth and age six.

Bruce H. Lipton, Ph.D., a pioneer in this new biology, is an internationally recognized leader in bridging science and Spirit. A cell biologist by training, Bruce was on the faculty of the University of Wisconsin's School of Medicine and later performed groundbreaking research at Stanford University. In his best-selling book, *The Biology of Belief,* he wrote, "The predominant brain activity during the child's first two years of life is delta, the lowest EEG frequency range. Between two and six years of age, the child's brain activity ramps up and operates primarily in the range of theta. While in the theta state, children spend much of their time mixing the imaginary world with the real world."

From birth to 2 years old, the human brain operates in delta mode, which is akin to sleeping or unconscious activities. From 4 to 6 years old, the brain is operating in theta mode, which activates imagination and reverie. They are programmable states of the brain, which means basically downloading information from the child's environment and all the experiences the child has during those early years.

By the ages of 6 to 12 years old, the brain is primarily in the range of alpha state, which is calm consciousness. This is a non-programmable state. By the age of 12 and beyond, the brain expresses all frequency ranges, although the primary activity is in the beta state, which is focused consciousness, also a non-programmable state. As children, we download our perceptions and beliefs about life years before we acquire the ability for critical thinking.

These brain states are a logical necessity during the formative stages of a child's life. The mind cannot operate from a blank slate. It requires a working platform of learned perceptions. Consequently, before we can express self-consciousness, the brain must go about acquiring a working awareness. A child's perceptions of the world are directly downloaded into the subconscious, without discrimination, and without filters of the analytical self-conscious mind, which doesn't fully exist. We download limiting or sabotaging beliefs, and those perceptions or misperceptions become our truths. Consequently, our fundamental perceptions about life and our role in it are learned without our having the capacity to choose or reject those beliefs. We were simply programmed. I call this "*The Writing on Our Wall.*"

The subconscious mind and the unconscious mind are largely invisible to us and it's interesting to note that our own subconscious and unconscious behaviors tend to cruise on autopilot. If our database is one of misperception, our subconscious mind will dutifully generate behavior patterns that are coherent with those programmed truths. Once programmed, that information would inevitably influence that individual's behavior for the rest of his or her life. This does not mean that we cannot change our minds—we can through the processes we will present in this book.

Where the conscious mind is creative, the subconscious mind only has a marginal aptitude for creativity. And while the conscious mind can express free will, the subconscious mind expresses only pre-recorded stimulus-response habits. The subconscious mind is simply an information processor that records all of our perceptual experiences and forever plays them back at the push of a button, like a tape recorder.

To avoid the shame and blame game, it is important to remember that the information has been recorded as a function of the workings of the brain. The *writing on our wall* has been downloaded indiscriminately from the words and actions of others who were no doubt programmed with many of the same limiting beliefs. Interestingly enough, we only become aware of our subconscious mind's button-pushing programs when someone else *"pushes our buttons."*

What happens when somebody pushes our buttons and we get triggered? Actually, the entire image of pushing buttons is far too slow and linear to describe the awesome data processing capacity of the subconscious mind. Once we learn a behavior pattern, such as walking, getting dressed, or driving a car, our brain relegates these programs to the subconscious mind. For example, when we get in our car, we no longer need to remember to put on our seat belt, put the key in the ignition, check the mirrors, put the car in drive, etc. We do these actions as if we are doing them automatically without thinking about them because we have done them so frequently that our brain now regulates these tasks to the subconscious mind. How many times have you driven down the same road and were unaware that you were even driving? So often in fact that you hardly pay attention and cannot believe how quickly the time passed while your mind was thinking about something other than the drive.

The subconscious mind has awesome data processing capabilities interpreting and responding to some 40 million plus nerve impulses per second. Whereas the conscious mind, located in the pre-frontal cortex, only processes about forty nerve impulses per second. This means, as an information processor, the subconscious mind is one million times faster and more powerful than the conscious mind. This answers our original question—Why do we do what we do and why do we keep doing that?

The subconscious mind controls every behavior that is not attended to by the conscious mind, which is just about everything in present time! For most of us, the conscious mind is so preoccupied about the past, the future, or some imaginary problem, that we leave the day-to-day, moment-to-moment tasks to the subconscious mind.

Scientists have concluded that the conscious mind contributes only 5% of our cognitive activity. This means the subconscious mind is controlling our decisions, emotions, actions, and behaviors 95% of the time. So, if we are operating from the subconscious mind 95% of the time, and the information stored on the subconscious data bank was programmed between the ages of 0 to 6, we might ask ourselves how it feels to have a 4-year-old driving our bus!

Many of us occasionally feel that we are of two minds about something—that we are conflicted. The mind that had the idea is the conscious mind, the one with the 40-bit processor. It's the part of the mind that creates, wants, desires, and sets intentions. It's the part we really must pay attention to because it's the part of the mind that imagines who we think we are, and yet it only controls 5% or less of our lives!

With our subconscious mind running the show 95% of the time, our fate is actually under the control of our recorded programs or habits we may not even know about or that are not of our own choosing. The *"writing on our wall"* is again a term I use to describe the downloaded information and programming that is recorded on the subconscious mind.

What is fascinating is that we check the *writing on our walls* for every experience much like a tape machine with tracks; the tracks on the subconscious mind are what we call neuropathways. When we have an experience, the subconscious mind checks the *writing on the wall* for programming from a similar past experience and says, "Oh yeah, we know what to do here." And off we go to do the thing we do, often without our awareness. We are habitually reacting, taking action, or performing some kind of behavior to every experience we encounter based on this automatic programming.

So, who's controlling our subconscious programming? There is no entity in the brain to control our subconscious programs. It's the mind, not the brain, that tells the body what to do. We can self-talk using reason to communicate with and try to change our subconscious and it will only have the same effect as trying to change a program on a cassette tape by talking to the tape player. In either case, there is no entity or component within the mechanism of the brain that will respond to our dialogue.

The good news is that we can transform the trance using Emotional Intelligence. Our willpower and our intentions need a new pathway. To create this new pathway, we will need to examine what's *written on our wall*. These subconscious programs are not fixed and unchangeable.

We do have the ability to rewrite our limiting beliefs and, in the process, take control of our lives.

Throughout this book you will be introduced to ways you can engage in what is called a self-discovery process to determine what is *written on your wall.* You will also be given the tools for practicing Awareness and Emotional Intelligence to assist you in transforming the old programming into what is really true for you.

These processes will assist you in navigating through the many aspects of life, especially those aspects that cause us anxiety, stress, and pain. It is important to remember that others who *wrote on our wall* did so unknowingly, as they were in turn programmed by other factors such as culture, society, religion, old beliefs, etc., backward through time. The stories from our ancestral history, along with our ancestor's comments and any conclusions they passed on to us, it's all *written on our walls* and yet it is only a story we keep telling our self. It is only their experience in a different time and place. With this understanding, we are able to shift from the blame game to responsibility—our responsibility is our ability to respond. The reality is that there is no good/bad, right/wrong, shame/blame. Every experience simply "is as it is." It's all about our unique perspective and it's coming from the *writing on our wall.*

The Mind is the Map

PART I: THE PROCESS

FINDING JOY

I — Understanding Our Patterns
II — Our Life Force Energy
III — Awareness is the Compass
IV — The Critical Voice ... The Writing on Our Wall
V — Emotional Intelligence
VI — The Mind is Not Free to be Happy
VII — The Present Moment
VIII — Hiding our Emotions in Prison
IX — Creating a New Experience
X — Learning to Live Lightly
XI — Living Life with Passion
XII — Creating Our New Story

PART II: CULTIVATING THE JOURNEY

The Mind is the Map

PART I: THE PROCESS

Understanding Our Patterns

I

FINDING JOY

While working towards understanding our patterns, make no attempt to suffocate any emotions because our emotions are not only powerful, but also trustworthy. Make an effort to locate the emotion's underlying essence, acknowledge its reality, test its origin, and separate its productive energy.

All too often man ignores the wisest command ever given
by a sage, the famous
"Know Thyself" *inscribed in the temple of Delphi.*

CHAPTER ONE

UNDERSTANDING OUR PATTERNS

CR: SO MUCH of living a full and happy life is about knowing ourselves. And both the forming and the breaking of patterns is a lifelong learning practice. The path to higher levels of understanding who we are requires us to discern the patterns that are shaping our lives. Discovering which ones will sustain us, and which ones no longer benefit us, as well as which ones we might want to create, are important to understand.

By the time we are adults, we have so much writing on our walls and we have so many old wounds from unresolved experiences that many of our responses are automatically negative. They perpetuate events that are not the best outcome and instead, they serve only to reinforce our initial learning from a time long ago. We get caught in a negative emotional event cycle often based on long forgotten past memories.

Because of the speed and bandwidth of the subconscious mind, the mind gets hijacked and once the mind is hijacked, it is running with these negative cycles of our earlier programming and we find that these past negative events create negative emotional reactions. They become more and more frequent until the originating event is healed. Some of these reactions continue to trigger negative interactions and might include judgment of self or others, feelings of being the victim, comparing our self to others, as well as a perception that we are not all equal, and so many more.

As we delve into what it means to live with patterns, we need look no further than the story of our own lives unfolding. Often there is constant tension, as we are continuously creating patterns to make sense of our lives as we become aware of our habitual patterns. The goal is not to eliminate the tension. No, in fact that is impossible because we are always forming, sustaining, and breaking down patterns. We are always being born again, living and dying in some form. Actually, the tension is helpful in revealing the patterns and learning how to hold onto those which sustain life, while transforming those that no longer serve us.

Upon examining the nature of our patterns, we need to discern the healthy ones—those that we practice mindfully from the unhealthy ones of our habitual routines. What we can do is soften our habitual routines back into mindful and meaningful practices. The rigid, sharp-edged ones need to be softened or broken so our hearts can be at peace. This softening and breaking of patterns is not about eliminating our humanness and it's not about eliminating our emotions, wants, and desires. It is about curbing the stubborn ways we hurt and disrespect ourselves and others. So often we go looking for ourselves where we are not.

It is not helpful to criticize ourselves, or to label our patterns as good or bad, and then try to rid ourselves of them. The aim is not to make ourselves pure and one-sided in living our lives, but it is to be authentically our self, learning what our strengths and weaknesses are. It's about learning how to live in the rhythm of being human and to celebrate ourselves and others as the magical imperfect individuals that we are.

Self-reflection and self-realization are tools we can use to cleanse and become our transparent self—the one who feels both joy and pain and the one that feels everything that moves us through life. We practice self-realization because the self is the only way through which we can experience life and our place in the world. What actually saves us from our self and our patterns is the power of our own honest gaze. We all get triggered by various experiences, and we can process these experiences from our thinking mind through a compass we call Awareness. We cannot will these disturbing emotions away. Instead, we must learn to accept them and process them by living through them from our heart as a way of living mindfully in peace.

Emotional Intelligence is another tool we can use and it is something we can learn to do with practice. Struggling with our feelings and emotions by applying logic and reason will not be helpful once the mind has been hijacked. From the point of noticing the trigger, and before the emotions become overwhelming, we have only a few seconds to step into heart Awareness. This is an important topic and we will expand on this process of Awareness in another chapter in this work.

Another interesting thing happens once the mind has been hijacked. All the systems of the body move into action releasing chemicals to support us while in an overwhelmed state. This is why it is not helpful to continue trying to communicate while we are overwhelmed or to communicate with someone who is already overwhelmed. The helpful information comes from the conscious mind. Once the mind has been hijacked, we are locked into our old patterns from the subconscious mind until we come out of the state of being overwhelmed. To override this internal struggle, we need to move into Awareness and process the experience and our emotions from the heart.

In recent years, scientists have discovered that the heart has its own independent nervous system; a complex system referred to as "*the brain in the heart.*" This system receives and relays information back to the brain in the head, creating a two-way communication between the heart and the brain.

There is another interesting read on this topic, which is *The Inner Voice of Love*, by Henri Nouwen. He writes, "The great challenge is living your wounds through instead of thinking them through. It is better to cry than to worry, better to feel your wounds deeply than to understand them, better to let them enter your silence than to talk about them. The choice we all face constantly is whether we are taking our hurts to our head or to our heart. In our head, we can analyze them, find their causes and consequences, and coin words to speak and write about them. But no final healing is likely to come from that source. We need to feel our emotions fully; let our wounds go down into our heart. Then allow ourself to live them thoroughly and we will discover that they will not destroy us. Our heart is greater than our wounds."

Life is role playing. The story has been written and now we need to study the script and do the work of endless rehearsals when our patterns keep revealing themselves to us, learning the lessons we came here to learn. Patterns are like this—until the lesson is learned, it will automatically repeat itself, often without our even knowing. Every day we are offered many chances to practice seeing our patterns simply by being in relationship to the many forms of life that feed us, that mirror us, and connect us. As with many things that matter in life, we must know ourselves well and we must face life, despite the countless distractions, obstacles and our patterns, as life is our journey.

We have to let go of the mind's need to stay in control of our pain and trust in the healing power of our heart. Going to our heart with our wounds or any incomplete experiences we may have is not easy. We must take our questions to the heart. In our discovery process, for example, we want to know, "Why was I wounded? When? How? By whom?" The answers to these questions will come from the mind and although they may help us to understand ourselves better, at best, they only offer us a little distance from our pain.

True healing happens as we continue our inner work of seeing and transforming our patterns. With humility and awe, we find ourselves living a more curious journey—perhaps even a journey back to innocence, back to the beginning. The closer we get to the truth and beauty of who we are, the more authentic and beautiful we become. As we move through the distractions and obstacles, reconfiguring our habitual patterns, we become clear vessels and it becomes easier to merge with the rhythm of all that is. It is here where we discover some mysterious laws of inner alchemy. The closer we get to the light, the more fully we become the light. It is in this moment we find out once and for all who we really are.

Dimitrios Spanos (DS): Christina, it amazes me as to how we as a species have collected incredible amounts of data, and studied and learned so much about our Earth, planets, and the Universe. And although we have spent hundreds of years understanding all kinds of natural phenomenon, we have not been able to fully understand the workings of our own mind and eliminate our own negative habitual patterns in order to bring total happiness and joy into our lives.

Living a life of completeness and wholeness requires us to find the source of our emotions and transform our wounds so we discover our true potential.

Caring for our soul requires that we become sensitive to any parts that are rough and begin to polish patterns that are rigid.

Kindness is our loving Spirit in action, and if we are to be kind to the outside world, we must first be kind to our self and transform our fixed and inflexible ways.

When we look deeply within us and become aware of our own loveliness and beauty, we can then allow our pristine mind to detect the dry and rugged patterns and nourish these with images of purity and illumination.

CR: Yes, Dimitrios, it is our destiny to fully immerse ourselves in the great experience called life and to live a self-approved life in harmony with the Universe, where we claim our Divine birthright to create our best life.

Some people don't want to revisit their experiences and perhaps a deeper reason is that they really don't want others to understand them completely, seemingly wanting to be invisible and to go through life unknown to themselves or others. They may truly feel that this blindness provides them safety and freedom. However, life is meant to be lived and experienced fully. With this mindset, they are only able to live a very small part of the reality of who they are and why they are here. When they live a very small and limited part of who they really are, they become unsatisfied with the life they are imagining and creating for themselves and may say things like, "What happened to my life?" or "Is this all there is?"

We hear a lot about living in the present moment, but few actually grasp the full meaning of this statement. Perhaps to fully comprehend it, we need to fully understand our self and to do that, we need to engage in the self-discovery process and the process of creation.

We can learn to understand the mind is the map, do our discovery work, and transform our habitual behaviors, thus beginning this process where we are in the present moment—not in the past nor in the future. Only from the present moment can we engage in the process of change and create a new direction in our life.

Change always requires a choice and there are no choice points in the past or the future. It can only be found in the present moment. Change does not need to happen with the loud drama that we often hear about. In truth, it is often experienced as unbelievably soft. Often, the experience of change is not even noticed until a special moment when our life is filled with a new light and loving essence that is very hard to miss.

We have discussed perceptions and some of our patterns and where they come from. These next few chapters are an invitation to know ourselves better, to understand what contributes to making us more authentic, and in doing so, will move us closer to our destiny. We will introduce some processes for transforming the patterns that no longer work for us. We will discover only one real destiny and one genuine vocation and that is to find the way to self, "To know thyself." The journey may be long, but it is the worthiest of all journeys. The path toward self-awareness is an initiation to finding and living one's highest self.

*

Going Deeper

CR: Our patterns are part of our human experience. When a pattern is triggered by an experience, we feel it by way of our emotions, and we habitually react to it and allow it to influence decisions that have important consequences for all our lives. Understanding our emotions and patterns can be considered a form of art requiring skill, awareness, and creativity. The starting point is not struggling with the pattern. Instead, fully accept what is occurring and remain open to sensing the freedom of change. This is easier said than done. It takes a lot of practice to remain open to intense emotions without our habitual responses of defending our territory.

Staying open, we can relax in the midst of emotional upheaval and appreciate it for what it is. How we experience this openness depends on the situation and our perceptions of it. By accepting that we have been triggered and opening up to the situation, we can pay attention to our feelings and our surroundings; sensing what is needed with an open mind and heart. This will help us to discriminate between reacting from our habitual patterns and move us toward more useful and mindful responses.

Acknowledging that sometimes our past responses did not work very well for us, we start from the present moment and look for its creative potential. We reconsider the situation and we look at the details from various perspectives and with fresh eyes—remaining sensitive to our feelings. The questions below are not always easy to answer and many beginners at this process of self-discovery feel frustrated. My suggestion is to try turning this frustration into genuine curiosity about getting to know yourself on a deeper level. Remain curious and play with the mystery and wonder of all that is.

Ask yourself these discovery questions:

How often do I react to people and situations based on old habits (perceiving, thinking, feeling, behaving)?

Have you ever noticed how you become defensive? Before even realizing it, you automatically respond as if those old experiences were happening again (defense mechanisms). All of us have developed habitual patterns of behavior and all automatic reactions are based on past experiences.

What is it that is actually bothering me? What patterns do I see?

What do I feel about these patterns?

What triggers me?

What habitual behavior patterns do I engage in when I have been triggered?

What do I believe about myself or about others (consciously or subconsciously) which is forcing me to behave in this manner?

What may have happened in the past which may have programmed me to have these beliefs?

Which patterns do I want to change that are now causing my pain or unhappiness?

What is my lesson here? What do I need to learn?

How can I make this change in my mental emotional processes?

Journaling

CR: Begin a journal about your experience. Notice how your life might be driven by undesirable habitual patterns? See any fight and/or flight patterns you might act out in your reactions. See how you react, attack, and become defensive. Determine how you might get hooked on by these habits. These patterns keep going all the time and cause destruction everywhere. Through journaling, we begin to practice the art of discovery. We learn to recognize our habitual patterns, discover how they affect us and those around us, and learn to work with them. Do not try to solve all the pattern problems in this exercise. Instead, simply allow yourself time to process them and allow more questions to come up. Our patterns, thoughts, and beliefs with our relationships to our families, our wealth, our society, and ourselves have caused us many problems and suffering. Learning to identify and work with these habitual patterns is the key to transforming our lives.

Here are three steps to assist the process of transformation:

1. Notice what you are doing. Pay attention to how you respond habitually to any event in your life.
2. Do something different. Consider responding to the experience in a very different way. This will loosen up the pattern.
3. Make it a way of life. Keep doing something different. This will bring about your own wisdom, strength, and fundamental goodness of the heart and mind.

Connect with Others

CR: Start a conversation with a friend or loved one sharing your experiences and your insights from your journaling. Do active listening while encouraging the other person to tell their story of where they are on the discovery of their patterns. Reflect with your friend or partner on both stories and discuss any missed opportunities to choose a better response when triggered. Discuss how needs, attachments or beliefs, might have interfered with a more favorable response. How might you have made a different choice rather than your habitual patterned response?

Milestones

CR: Few of us have a very intimate knowledge of our patterns. By accepting our undesirable habitual patterns, we can learn to gently and skillfully work with them, soften our sharp edges, and gain confidence in our ability to respond to our experiences with wisdom. Our negative habitual patterns turn from compost to fertile ground where we can plant new seeds of Awareness. Each time you discover a pattern accurately, you have reached another milestone. Celebrate these milestones by recognizing them and slow down to take a moment to feel what is true for you instead of simply answering with an automatic habitual response.

Making it Personal

DS: The wisdom of the Universe keeps re-creating our Earth, engaging all of us in a cosmic dance with God. Nature as a master artist conceives intricate patterns in plants, flowers, and crystals. On the other hand, we, just like nature, develop complex patterns in our way of living.

While many of our habitual patterns have a positive contribution and ascend us to higher levels of consciousness, others make us suffer and deplete our energy. In order to live a joyous and balanced life, we must become aware of any undesirable habitual patterns and figure out ways to transform them.

Starting from a young age we form our language, imagination, and creativity. Information that comes from the outside environment, parents, school teachers, and others, along with the collective unconscious, shapes our core beliefs. Afterwards, these beliefs get stored as *writings on our walls* and if triggered by a new event, sometimes much later in life, they facilitate our automated programmed responses.

Our behaviors are the result of these complicated belief structures. Reality is different for each one of us, but how we perceive reality is how we create reality. The question is that of consciousness. The more conscious we are, the closer we get to reality. In order to do so, we need to keep examining our beliefs and assumptions, and we need to transform them to ones that serve us better—ones that can lead us towards living happier more peaceful lives.

During self-discovery, I noticed a number of external events that would influence my thoughts and emotions not always for the better. In addition, certain decisions kept me from seeing greater opportunities for growth.

I asked myself, "Why was I making these limited decisions?

What did I believe about the experience that kept limiting me?

Was I acting on old childhood conclusions that were not helpful?"

It appeared that whatever beliefs I had previously accepted as reality, no longer served their function and kept causing me discomfort and emotional pain. This untransformed emotional energy kept moving my body from hot to cold and light to heavy while some of the internal sensations felt like winter chills, moist-like spring rains, and hot feelings just like the mid-summer sun. It was time to find balance and create better choices.

I asked myself, "What was it from the past that kept influencing the present?

How did my past experiences keep creating automatic modes of my reactions?

Why do I believe what I believe?

Did I intentionally choose those beliefs or was I just following opinions and ideas of others?

What beliefs do I need to transform to achieve my dreams and bring the utmost happiness in my life?

How could I overcome the pre-conceived experiences of my mind's programming and take full responsibility for my own thoughts and feelings?

What would it take to stop blaming the outside world and to stop overreacting to different issues?

What were the triggers that kept causing major hardship to my life?

What kind of activities was I involved in when these triggers took place?

What outside events were connected with these triggers?

Was I flexible enough to create more possibilities and choices in my behaviors?"

I kept observing and questioning any limited beliefs, triggers, and automatic responses in order to raise the level of my awareness. In my effort to understand the process of undesired thoughts and unwanted emotions, one thing became crystal clear. It was that I could never blame the outside world for what I was feeling. I am the only one in my mind. I am its whole creator, host, and owner.

Emotional hijacking is a very unpleasant feeling and a state of mind where we feel that we are no longer in charge of our own thoughts and emotions. During these times, we might feel that someone has misunderstood us, treated us unfairly, and thus we may feel that our choices are limited. In such cases, we might lose self-control or we might feel overwhelmed by our emotions. At this point, the mind has become emotionally hijacked.

Hijacking of the mind feels like an outside attack, where the perpetrator seems to take illegal control of something of ours and we need to defend it. What is really happening is that our rational mind is overloaded by our emotions and interferes with our reasoning. What is remarkable is that during the hijacking process, our mind is taken over in less than six seconds, which is almost the same rate of a full inhale and exhale. However, no matter how little six seconds may sound, we still have a choice not to give up. The reason for this is that many things can take place during that period of time. In six seconds, hundreds of thousands of reactions are happening in our body and it's interesting to note that within six seconds, a bee can flap its wings more than one thousand times!

An example of this hijacking is anger and it can range from mild to rage. It happens very quickly and while we are on the emotional rollercoaster, we bounce up and down, left and right, seemingly without any self-control. It should be noted that there is validity in using anger. For instance, controlled anger can instill confidence. However, losing control under the emotion of anger leads to stress, anxiety, and hostility and makes it difficult to focus on how we would like to respond to the event happening in the present moment.

While working towards understanding the pattern of anger, I made no attempts to suffocate the emotion because our emotions are not only powerful, but also trustworthy. My effort was to locate the emotion's underlying essence, acknowledge its reality, test its origin, and separate its productive energy.

The Habitual Pattern of Getting Angry

How do you deal with interruptions? I used to get angry each time I was interrupted while talking. For example, the trigger kicked in during meetings when a member of my team jumped up and tried to finish my sentence in an attempt to push their own agenda. I would feel that their action was completely unnecessary and the interruption not only caused loss in my train of thoughts, but also it would lower the quality of my expression.

While I was under the influence of uncontrolled anger, the speed and volume of my speech increased and soon afterwards, I would use loud verbalizations. In addition, the negative thoughts going through my mind kept creating an emotional blockage that made me feel frustrated and irritated.

In order to remember the intensity of what triggered this anger, I named it the "agitated interruption anger (AIA)" and focused on understanding the stream of thoughts and images arising from the emotional hijacking.

I questioned myself and asked the following:

"What was the need I had that was not met and, therefore, making me angry?

What was my belief underneath this anger?

What were my thoughts and corresponding behaviors and reactions?

How did my physiology change during the anger?

What were the underlying sensations?

How was the energy of anger pulling me away from the present moment?

What was the purpose of my anger?

Was I being effective while being angry?

Did getting angry get me what I really wanted?

When I got triggered, what limited beliefs obscured the natural state of my mind?

How did my old wounds influence this kind of anger?"

While focusing on the above questions, I worked towards building the capacity of slowing down the reactive process of anger and regulating its energy. Our emotions are warning signs that can be used in a beneficial way. The choice to react or act in any certain situation is always ours and our soul desires to be able to make more conscious decisions with appropriate responses.

Life's demands will always create triggers for most of us. Recognizing the energy and corresponding internal sensations associated with our triggers helps us to avoid unhealthy reactions. Understanding and using our triggers as a map of our mind will effectively teach us more about ourselves and the programming beneath our habitual tendencies. We can then shift our habitual patterns towards a new way of living our life lightly and wholly.

The Mind is the Map

PART I: THE PROCESS

Our Life
Force
Energy

II

III   IV

Understanding
Our
Patterns

I

**FINDING
JOY**

So many people today are chasing success and
sacrificing their time, their relationships, and their
sanity to get "there" at any cost, without even
considering the cost of their Life Force Energy.
Have you ever stopped to think about how
you define your level of Life Force Energy?
You should!

PART II:

CULTIVATING THE JOURNEY

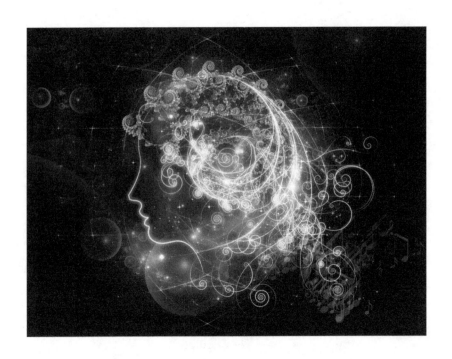

Einstein's Paradigm:

*"You cannot solve a problem from the same consciousness
that created it. You must learn to see the world anew."*

CHAPTER TWO

OUR LIFE FORCE ENERGY

CR: "WHAT STRANGE BEINGS WE ARE!" noted the 13th Century mystic, Rumi. The bigger question might be, "Are we here to live passive lives, using the old programmed templates of our ancestors, or can we really create our own lives?" Today, scientific evidence suggests that we are creators of our own reality and that it is *our consciousness* that holds the key to our health, life, and even reality itself. As humans, we are receivers and transmitters of the cosmic Life Force Energy. Our body, mind, feelings, thoughts, intentions, conditioned responses, inner conflicts, and any unresolved emotional pain are all energy, and all energy is connected to all other energy.

Life Force Energy is exactly what it sounds like. It is the Universal Energy that gives life to all things. Our thoughts are energy and give rise to our emotions, which in turn are simply energy in motion like invisible clouds hovering above and around our physical body. High frequency emotions, such as love and joy, are bright, while lower frequency emotions are dimmer and sometimes dark.

Negative or lower frequency emotions such as hate, humiliation, blame, despair, regret, anxiety and other emotions can have a detrimental effect on our physical body over time. These emotions eventually can become toxic at the cellular level and can damage body tissues and even become serious diseases. Emotions are stored in the body in layers on top of layers and these can affect our mood, attitude, and personality in their degree of concentration. Some people, for example, are always very angry and others hardly angry at all.

We can allow our emotions to flow freely and we can also repress them. In order for us to be clear of lower frequency emotions from our emotional body, we need to release them. However, we can't release them by just saying, "OK, I release all my sadness right now!" It is the thoughts we think that are causing the emotions we feel and they can only be released in their energetic form. We can only let go and release them by transmuting them to higher energetic frequencies, and we do this by changing our thoughts. Changing our thoughts requires the practices of Awareness, Mindfulness, and Emotional Intelligence.

The entire Universe is made of pure energy; impersonal, unformed, and intelligent. This means that we are free to create whatever we desire while accepting the energetic consequences of our actions. Because of this, there is no need for us to judge anything or anyone. Our trust in the Universe means accepting each experience as it is and knowing that each person is on their own path, learning from their own choices.

The problem comes in because our human mind wants to classify things to understand them. Since we live in a world of duality of opposites, we see good or bad, right or wrong, shame or blame, etc. In fact, sometimes we cannot fully comprehend something without knowing its opposite. But we can transcend our mind and connect with our heart, enabling us to feel gratitude for our own partnership in cooperation with the Universe and the path we follow without judgment.

Each of us has our own unique energetic footprint. As energy beings, we vibrate our unique energetic footprint all the time. It is interesting that neither the old medical model nor the life scientists of the past considered this as it is one of the most fundamental and possibly least understood dynamics related to the energy field surrounding all of life.

All the world as we know it is ultimately made of light energy; tiny packets of light, known as quanta, vibrating at different speeds. Some light vibrates so slowly that it appears solid to us, such as material goods or rocks and minerals. Other forms of light vibrate more rapidly and appear to us as the living material of plants, animals, and people. Even faster vibrations make up our unseen television, radio, and microwave signals. Ultimately, each may be reduced to a quality of vibrating light.

Life Force Energy is what causes us to grow and it is this Life Force that enables us to heal ourselves. Some of us call it by other names such as Prana, Chi, or Spirit. It is the energy that evokes the true and only healing that comes from within. Most of us know that while a drug may relieve the symptoms of a disease, it does not cure the disease. A true cure always involves a shift in our Life Force Energy, brought about by a major change in the attitude towards self and towards life.

Life Force Energy enters our body through our breath and flows through the acupuncture meridians and vitalizes the organs and tissues. When the flow of this Life Force Energy is depleted or not in balance, this will ultimately lead to disease in the physical body. These depletions and imbalances come about as a result of physical and psychological factors. Through our mental powers, we have the ability to increase and rebalance the flow of Life Force Energy throughout the body and, thus, combat disease.

Our Life Force Energy is the blueprint, the infrastructure, the invisible foundation for the health of our body. Our body is composed of energy pathways and energy centers that are in a dynamic interplay with our cells, organs, moods, and thoughts. If we can shift these energies, we can shift our health, emotions, and state of mind. When we are filled with Life Force Energy, we are healthy, peaceful, and calm. It is the Spirit pervading the mind and body, which is the healing force within us.

DS: Yes, Christina, our Life Force Energy is our infrastructure. Nature's elements and the Universe provide our life-giving energy, animates our body, and channels it through our mind and soul. All forces of nature, sunlight, air, and wind are manifestations of the Life Force Energy and we, in turn, are a true reflection of their natural beauty.

We all experience the beauty and sustenance of nature. We get to see the sunshine each day; the reflection of light on Earth; the elegance of mountains; trees; the liveliness of the crystals; minerals; the blooming of flowers; and the ocean's rhythmic movement.

Our sun's light transforms our own light while our etheric body takes the sun's rays and creates energy and vitality for our physical cells. Our lungs take oxygen from the air and transports it through 60,000 miles of vessels to deliver it everywhere in our body in order to keep us alive. The spectacular and wondrous ebb and flow of the Life Force Energy creates a blissful harmony within our body circulating in our blood and influencing our breathing patterns.

CR: Thank you, Dimitrios. This lovely word picture truly depicts the flow of our Life Force Energy. Now that we understand that everything in our world is created of energy and this energy creates energetic footprints and fields of energy around each one of us, it is important to protect our own energetic field. One of the most difficult challenges in life is learning not to take things personally. There are times we feel overwhelmed by our emotions, especially when we are criticized or attacked by others. This is the result of allowing the negative energy of the other person, or the negative experience itself, to merge with our personal energy field. We must try not to take on the energy of others in an experience as our own. Sometimes there are numerous others involved in our experiences, all with opinions of their own, and often these conflicts can cause even more misunderstandings. This only exasperates the issues with so many opinions creating even more conflicting energy and issues in the larger scope of things.

Unfortunately, we cannot fix others. We can only learn to remain in our moment-to-moment interactions, holding a loving space for them as we ourselves continue on the path of self-realization. We must welcome the triggers in life as stepping stones to our own understanding of self and the wounds we need to heal. We sometimes lose our power by allowing others to change our Life Force Energy by reacting in a negative way when we are triggered. It is better to see the triggers as gifts to us, ones that tell us volumes about our self. When we are triggered, we will feel it as a pushback; an opportunity to go deeper into understanding the self. Our question is, "What is it within me that got triggered?" Any fluctuations, high or low, in our Life Force Energy is never about something or someone out there—it is always an inside job.

One of the precipitating factors causing energy imbalance is stress, physical or mental. The first sign of that stress will always show up as a reduction of Life Force Energy. Coincidental with stress, a specific negative emotional attitude will be created. It may be that of unhappiness, depression, anger, or any of the other negative emotions we experience.

By continually monitoring our mind/body states, and by using the processes we will outline in this book, we can shift any thoughts or emotions that are out of balance. We are able to maintain a high and balanced Life Force Energy and, thus, we remain healthy. By overcoming the negative emotional states, we are in a position to practice true prevention of disease in the body, not only preventing ourselves from being sick, but actually beginning to feel positively well.

Our Life Force Energy fluctuates up and down because there is a lot of crossover when dealing with emotions and feeling levels. As we work to improve our self-knowledge and our communication skills and reach new levels of understanding of both self and others, the Life Force Energy levels adjust themselves with new respect and new ways of connecting. Until that time, our interpersonal relationships are tangled, intertwined, and sometimes gnarled energy.

We stated earlier that our thoughts and feelings are energy, and that emotions are our "*energy in motion*." We have feelings about everything, whether we want to admit to them or not. It helps to remember that the energy of our emotions is connected to everything else. It does not matter what belongs to us and what belongs to them, or what he said or she said—we are all one and we are each responsible for how we respond to life and to each other. It's also interesting to note that our positive behavior helps raise the vibration of others involved in our experiences. The goal is to live life as much as possible from a place of love. Ask yourself often, "What would love do now?"

It has been said that there is a gift in every experience. Perhaps the mechanisms of how the mind works is the gift of a natural life lesson occurrence that continues to trigger us, thereby giving us opportunities to see our patterns, to process them, and to transform them. The self-discovery process and the use of the Awareness process helps to break the negative cycles and this is paramount in raising our emotional state to one of experiencing higher frequency vibrational emotions such as joy, love, acceptance, etc. We begin by making the decision, using our will, and our power to choose that we no longer wish to behave in this way.

Each of us are uniquely different on our path or journey in life and as such, it is better to show up with loving compassion in all of our experiences and under all circumstances. Most of the time, the attacks and criticisms of others have much more to do with the *writing on their wall*, something going on within them and how they are feeling, than it has to do with us. It is very easy to lose touch with our core, our center of unconditional love, when we get caught up in trying to adjust ourselves to other people's negative energy. If we react with a negative response, we only add to this negative energy field multiplying its effect for all.

There is NO separation from our body's energy, another body's energy, and the energy that is from the source of all that exists. There is only separation through our thoughts and language. Humanity's comprehension of the messages encoded through text and "implemented" through the rules and rituals that originate with the *writing on our walls* has us trapped in a box of beliefs—and the "box" is an illusion, the limit doesn't exist. Life, just as the Universe, is all connected, is ever evolving, expanding, and infinite. Life is the definition of consciousness itself, and we as human beings are the cosmos made conscious, and this lifetime is merely but a chapter in a story that never ends. We can all become masters of our energetic integrity, refusing to participate in anger and frustration and to always respond with loving kindness to ourselves and the people around us. With this practice, we will add only loving energy to the collective field of consciousness for all.

*

Going Deeper

CR: When caught in a lower vibrational frequency, things can seem hard to overcome. However, in today's world, we are fortunate to have many powerful tools, therapies, and valuable information available that can assist us. Choosing in a determined fashion to observe our self and how we react in stressful situations, and objectively looking at why we felt and reacted that way, thus seeking ways to dissolve any negative emotional hooks to past events empowers us to greatly improve our life experiences and to live a much happier life. When living in an emotionally higher vibrational state most of the time, our interactions with others dramatically improves. We are much happier and we attract to us more options and opportunities to live our best life.

No matter how overwhelmed, stressed, angry, or anxious we might feel during challenging moments, we have within us an innate power to change the way we approach these challenges by simply shifting our thoughts. Some of our emotional releases can be very painful. Because of that, we often tend to repress them deep within, not wanting to feel them again. No matter how intense and painful a release might be, we feel much better afterwards. The more we clear ourselves from accumulated lower frequency emotions, the higher our frequency will rise and the happier we'll become.

Journaling

CR: Begin a journal about your Life Force Energy's experience. Be sure to answer the questions below in great detail. Next write about an experience you had—one where you could feel your Life Force Energy at a low point. Include the emotions you felt at that time. As you write, feel the difference in your energy field. Next, write about an experience you had—one where you could feel your Life Force Energy at a very high point. Again, record any emotions you were feeling and once again feel the difference in your energy field.

If you want to live a powerful life, you have to ask powerful questions.

Here are just a few questions to consider:

What is the highest and best use of my energy? In today's busy world, time seems to be the one commodity we all are yearning for. But in order to feel like we're making the most of our Life Force Energy, we must first know what matters most to us. When you get clear and prioritize what's most important to *you*, you won't feel so trapped by lower level energies.

How do I define my own energetic vibrational footprint? So many people today are chasing success and sacrificing their time, their relationships, and their sanity to get "there" at any cost, without even considering the cost of their Life Force Energy. Have you ever stopped to think about how *you* define your level of Life Force Energy? Before you set out on your next big journey toward success, be sure to define what it looks like to you first. Then feel into your vision of your success. Using your imagination, try on different scenarios, and see what each one feels like from an energetic point of view.

Will my choices give me energy or deplete my energy? For everything you think, do or say in life, ask these questions.

What are my blind spots or areas of improvement? List areas in your current life or style of living where you might be losing or leaking your Life Force Energy.

How do I think that I might be standing in my own way? List some things you might want to change that are draining your Life Force Energy. Ignoring your Life Force Energy can be dangerous. It can cause us to become ill; stay in a relationship too long; or keep us stuck in a business or job that doesn't quite feel right. Whenever you feel torn or confused about how to increase your Life Force Energy with a particular situation, ask yourself what you're pretending not to know. Once you get your answer, be bold enough to listen to it and take action.

What am I grateful for? Maintaining a state of gratitude sends out a vibrational signal to the Universe to bring more of that into our lives. Gratitude is a higher form of Life Force Energy. Lower vibrational frequencies such as fear, scarcity, and doubt simply cannot live in a grateful heart. So, if you're experiencing the lower energy vibration of pain or discomfort, the easiest way to shift out of it is to ask yourself what you're grateful for. This will help you relax and increase your Life Force Energy.

How can I hold the space for increasing my Life Force Energy? It helps to remember that we create our own reality. Whatever "negative" things you are currently experiencing, something about your way of being initially welcomed them in. Remember our physics lessons, "like energy attracts like energy;" well our energetic footprint will attract to us like a magnet what we already are. We don't get what we want; we get what we are. If you don't like the reality you're living in, you must be brave enough to change something internally. After getting clear about how YOU are the space for what is occurring in your life, if you want to find an evolved solution to almost any problem, sit on this question and see what solutions come up —"What would love do right now?"

Be prepared not to have all the questions or answers. Remain open. Our tendency is to try to solve all the problems rather than allowing ourselves to have time to process and allow more questions to come up. Although it may seem inefficient, even when we feel sure that we have the answer in our mind, it is often best to complete the journal entry with a question rather than an answer. This question will then work in the subconscious mind calling forth answers, intuition (tuition from within), inspiration, and guidance from within.

Connect with Others

CR: Start a conversation with a friend or loved one sharing your experience and your insights from your journaling. Do active listening while encouraging the other person to tell their stories related to their Life Force Energy. Reflecting with your friend or partner on both stories, discuss any missed opportunities to make choices that raise our energy field and see how any needs, attachments, or beliefs might have interfered. We'll never truly be able to see ourselves objectively; therefore, we need to look outside of ourselves to get honest feedback about how we're showing up in life. Turn to those around you for an unbiased review. You can ask them, "What are my blind spots or areas of improvement? How do you think I'm most in my own way?" The key is to ask with a genuine curiosity to want to learn more about how others see you so that you can improve yourself.

Milestones

CR: Many people believe they are merely helpless victims of their circumstances. But in actuality, our external circumstances are the direct result of our Life Force Energy being directed by either our conscious or subconscious intent to create our exact life circumstances. Few of us have a very intimate contact with our Life Force Energy. When someone asks what we are feeling, we often answer vaguely, "bad, unhappy, upset, disturbed, and negative." We want to get more specific when describing our emotional state and we also want to feel into our energy level. Each time you take a moment to feel into your energy and name the emotions accurately that either heightened or lowered your energy level, you have reached another milestone. Celebrate these milestones by recognizing them and slow down to take a moment to feel what is true for you instead of simply answering with an automatic habitual response. Try feeling things fully on all levels: emotional, physical, and energetic.

Making it Personal

DS: We are permeated by a Universal Force Energy that is our Life Force Energy. Everything in the Universe moves to the natural rhythm of this Life Force Energy, which in turn is connected to our consciousness and acts as the carrier of our feelings and sacred meanings.

The Life Force Energy lives within us and around us and always vibrates at the highest frequency. The Life Force Energy is responsible for the flow of blood inside our arteries and veins and sustains our body's immunity. The kinetic aspect of this energy is responsible for our movement. We are always free to experience the Life Force Energy inside our head, hand, eye, arm, breast, and heart as a vehicle to consciousness and awareness. Working with the Life Force Energy keeps us connected to our spirit and unconditional love.

The Life Force Energy flows within us and around us and vibrates at a high frequency. Frequency is the rate of speed at which our essence vibrates. Each time we take a breath, we are inhaling frequency and when we tune our breath and body to the Life Force Energy, we move into its vibrational field. The flow of Life Force Energy will heal us from the adversity of life and draw us into meaning and purpose.

I have been connected to the Life Force Energy since my birth. By taking my first breath of life, I instinctively aligned with its power and received its everlasting abundance. As a child, I was magically connected to its natural flow, living within the Earth's sacred grounds, and playing in her gorgeous backyard. The Life Force Energy followed me in my childhood, sharing its power with everyone, filling their hearts with pleasure, joy, and cheerfulness.

Our thoughts and feelings are energy that vibrates and not only do they create our reality, they affect our Life Force Energy upwards or downwards, from higher to lower vibrations. This spiral movement will either have a positive or negative effect in our body, mind, and immune system.

Love is one of the highest forms of our Life Force Energy and love's vibration resonates as one of the highest energy frequencies. Love's transcendent power keeps raising our soul and the souls of those we love. Love that flows through me and you permeates everything to become a sacred union of love's presence at a higher frequency.

Love is not easy to define, but it is our biggest and greatest investment on Earth. The wealth of life is expressed in the memories of the people we love and those memories of events become markers of our journey.

Our desire to love and be loved is deeply imprinted within us. Keeping the gift of love flowing requires making deposits into the love bank. We love others and expect others to love us back. But what happens when someone, and especially a close family member, does not express their love feelings back to us? Do we hold our own feelings back, or do we feel rejected and turn cold?

In a healthy relationship, positive energy flows all the time. However, negative energy can prevent love to grow and flourish. This is what was happening a few years ago while I was going through a difficult relationship with a beloved family member. Unfortunately, there was a lot of arguing, blaming, and criticizing. The emotional turmoil was not only creating a painful situation for both of us, but at the same time, was depleting the levels of our Life Force Energy making some of these levels stagnant and others like currents of rough and turbulent waters.

I examined my own energetic footprint and the energy of our relationship and asked the following questions:

What were the levels of my energetic balance, personal energy, and the energy of the other person in this relationship?

What were the demands and events that kept depleting the energy and vitality of our relationship?

What kind of thoughts and emotions were depleting the Life Force Energy?

What was needed from me to create a space for trust and unconditional love to grow?

Through this realization, I came to understand that the unkind and unproductive blaming and criticizing had to stop. I started to take responsibility for my own actions and thoughts and started to work towards reconciliation and healing. This meant shifting all negative thoughts and feelings to the loving capacity of the heart.

Next, I asked myself, "What action steps can I take to increase the Life Force Energy in my body and soul?"

I worked towards raising my own personal vibration and reconnected to the high frequency of the Life Force Energy that I had enjoyed as a child. Living in this higher vibrational state, my interaction with my beloved family member dramatically improved.

In order to offer greater support in the relationship, I moved my own feelings to a place of pure intent and focused on thoughts of love, appreciation, and encouragement. During conflicting situations, I imagined myself to be like a lamp holder of light, keeping the space of our love illuminated, and away from any suffering or discomfort.

All loving thoughts and actions brought a higher level of energy and soon enough, we were making deposits to the love bank. We were able to distance ourselves from the previous negative cycles of conflict. It wasn't long before we created a mission statement that included a host of intention statements. Together we set the foundation and guidelines towards a better and stronger relationship.

During the course of our life, we encounter life-changing events and get involved in relationships that move us out of our comfort zone. These events deplete our Life Force Energy. When our mind gets fixated on our own self-serving needs, we will need to raise our personal energetic footprint and reconnect with the frequency of love by aligning the energetic rhythms of our thoughts and feelings that are associated with the higher vibrations of the Life Force Energy.

The Mind is the Map

Awareness
is the
Compass

III   IV

FINDING
JOY

We can learn through Awareness to process our
thoughts, beliefs, and emotions through our hearts,
bypassing the mind stuff, enabling us to make
better choices on how we choose to respond to life.
We will be able to witness these aspects of every
experience, including seeing yourself from
an observer's point of view.

*"The ultimate value of life depends upon
Awareness and the power of contemplation
rather than upon mere survival."*

- Aristotle

CHAPTER THREE

AWARENESS IS THE COMPASS

CR: WE MUST learn to experience our self, free of the mind stuff, of our stories, and self-images. To experience our true self, we have to move away from the stories we have told our self about our self-image and any thoughts about our self in the experiences we are having right here and now in the present moment. We must be completely absent of thoughts and self-images, which obscure who we really are. As long as we continue to respond and react to our experiences with old ingrained emotional patterns and mechanisms, we will continue to feel the same emotions, continue to do what we have always done, and continue to attract the same behaviors and events. What we can do when we get triggered or we feel anxious is practice stepping into Awareness.

Many have asked, "What is Awareness?" Awareness is just itself—pure, alive, alert, silent, and full of potential. It is a feeling of being at ease with everything and everyone around us. It is a peace of mind and a sense of well-being, as well as an inner knowing that all is well, despite the circumstances we are in at the present moment. It is a feeling of being in control of our self within any experience, not in control of others, but of how we choose to respond to life.

Sometimes when we come close to experiencing this pure state, we begin to realize that our life has a purpose. Or we will sense that random events are not random, but form subtle patterns as witnessed in nature. We may realize that life has the ability to run itself and we might feel drawn to the center of all that is. If we notice even one hint such as this, we have in our hand a thread that could lead us beyond thought, feeling, or action. For there is only one reality and every clue must eventually lead to the same place, where the laws of creation operate freely, which is Awareness itself.

Consider Awareness as a place within us that allows us to see all aspects of our experiences, taking in all the varying perspectives, enabling us to create a more loving and conscious response to life. It is a state of mind where we become the observer of our self, of our feelings—a place where it is easy to understand the randomness and indiscriminating voice of the Ego's constant chatter or the constant wanting of something different than that which simply is. Practicing Awareness creates some distance from the egoic voice and allows us to see that we are free to choose whether to listen to it or not. We are better able to evaluate the wanting or desires and come to witness it for what it really is. We become clear and we are not affected by anything external to our being. We are immune to either criticism or praise. We understand that we are all equal and connected to the same consciousness and flow of the Universe.

As we shift into Awareness, we can feel there is another place within us that dwells in the silence of who we truly are. There is a place where the mind gives way and we are able to align ourselves to the intelligence beyond the thinking mind. This intelligence field creates for us physical, emotional, and spiritual balance. It is from this place we draw our true power and strength, giving us the flexibility to meet our challenges, and we are able to easily transform them in ways that are supporting and nurturing. This simple shift of our attention from the Ego's consistent chatter, criticism, and whining to the essence of our Spirit not only lessens our suffering, but increases our peace, contentment, joy, and happiness of our true essence. It is always found in the present moment. At this point, our Awareness is fully functioning, open to the novelty of sensing what the situation calls for.

When we are in Awareness, we become the observer of the mind, body, and the current experience we happen to be in and we can observe the subtle conversations between our mind and the body. This is one of the practices of Emotional Intelligence and using Emotional Intelligence in this way, we can have a profound impact that contributes to our wellbeing.

Understanding and dealing with our emotions is sort of a puzzle. In these first few chapters we discussed the tools and processes we can use and we will be pulling all these puzzle pieces together in more detail in the chapter called Emotional Intelligence.

We can learn through Awareness to process our thoughts, beliefs, and emotions through our hearts, bypassing the mind stuff, enabling us to make better choices on how we choose to respond to life. We will be able to witness the three aspects of every experience, including seeing yourself from an observer's point of view. The three aspects of Awareness are: self in the experience; the situation itself; and the manner in which self and others are processing the experience.

It helps to remember that we are not here to judge our self or others in the experience. We are only an observer. The others have nothing to do with our experience. No one can make us feel anything—not ever. Our feelings come from our thoughts and we are the only one in our mind. Simply observe what we are feeling. What we are telling our self, and what thoughts or beliefs might we have that may be creating any emotions and feelings within?

There is so much to see and ponder in every experience and when we step back from our experience and really see what's going on, we are acting from the heart. This is our true nature and it feels good to see everything from this perspective. For example, what might really be going on within the experience are two people who have been triggered, acting out the experience based on their individual perspective.

Often our programming has us making judgments, assumptions, and having us feel helpless or powerless in situations that seem hopeless. By acquiring a habit of stepping back, seeing and acting from a place of Awareness, it gives us the opportunity to see a new perspective of what's going on and it becomes an opportunity to re-evaluate and even rewire our habitual programming.

Here is a wonderful example of stepping into Awareness. In Eckhart Tolle's book, *The Power of Now*, Tolle describes a time in his life when he was going through such deep despair and torment that he considered suicide. Then a thought came to him, "exactly who is the "WHO" who wants to do away with whom?" At this moment, Tolle was in his Awareness. He was outside of the experience looking at it as a witness or observer of the experience and he could see clearly and as always, if we want the right answer, first we must ask the right questions!

When we are not in our Awareness, very often it is a signal to us that our subconscious childhood beliefs are not congruent with the beliefs we hold today as adults. For example: There is something we want to do, or something others are asking us to do, and that something is not a match with the *writing on our walls* from our subconscious mind. These conflicts cause us to become stressed and anxious and we tend to make poor decisions that compromise our effectiveness to respond in ways that are beneficial to us and to others. These conflicts occur because of the difference between who we are today and our learned and conditioned decisions, choices, and response behaviors. Our personal empowerment comes from discovering those differences and transforming our old childhood beliefs to ones that are aligned with positive conditioning, not from our default unconscious conditioning from old programming. We do this by stepping into Awareness.

While there are both conscious and unconscious conflicts, the conditioning at the basis of most inner conflicts is unconscious. Sometimes we know what our inner conflicts are. More commonly though, it seems that there are invisible forces keeping us from having the outcome we would like. This is because the inner conflict is typically coming from us unconsciously and automatically because the *writing on our wall* is consulted for everything we say and do. In both cases, the inner conflicts persist and we continue to suffer, usually without knowing why.

We cannot conduct conscious right actions while we are overwhelmed and engulfed by our emotions surrounding the experience. Remember how fast the processor is for the subconscious mind? We have only a few seconds from the moment we have been triggered to step into Awareness before the mind is hijacked and acts out our habitual programming. Once hijacked, we will need to hold a space for ourselves and others until the stress and anxiety caused by the emotions we are feeling have subsided or passed.

It's OK if we get hijacked—we all do! It helps to consider that we are learning a new process. This process takes lots of practice and life gives us plenty of opportunities to practice it. Our subconscious programs are not fixed, unchangeable behaviors. We have the ability to examine our limiting beliefs, redirect the mind to the heart and in the process, take control of our lives.

However, to control the mind's subconscious programs requires the activation of a process other than just engaging in a running dialogue with the subconscious mind. The use and practice of stepping into Awareness is engaging in Emotional Intelligence to assist us with our behavioral, habitual conditioning, and Energy Psychology techniques to help us to remove the electromagnetic charge, or in other words, the energetic footprint holding the habitual pattern in place. We have all been shackled with emotional chains wrought by dysfunctional behaviors programmed by the stories of the past. For example, if we grew up in an environment without a "loving model" from our caretakers, we may go through life feeling unloved or unworthy and unlovable. These patterns of behavior sometimes show up in our intimate relationships. We might find that we crave love and tend to look for love in all the wrong places. We might not have any appropriate boundaries or even deal breakers when it comes to loving another. Simply, we might not know how to love our self or another because we did not have a model for this as a child. All we have is the *writing on our wall* from our childhood. It might be that we learned from our caregivers what we don't want, and now as adults, we know what we do want, but our habitual patterns block our way to enjoying happy healthy relationships.

Understanding how the brain works and how our brain self-sabotages us and activates certain behaviors is one of the most exciting opportunities we will ever have because on the other side, is the emotional freedom and depth of joy that we were born to have. And the process of breaking through denial, facing our fears, anger, and other difficult emotions, and making peace with our pain, is going to lead us step-by-step into the greatest expression of our self.

*

Going Deeper

CR: Use the practice of Awareness to calm your mind when you find yourself on a vicious cycle of repeating patterns or of getting triggered by what someone says or does. It is also useful to quiet the negative voice in your head. When this happens, remember that you are the only one in the experience who can initiate change, and for goodness sake, STOP peddling and move into Awareness.

Think about any experience you are having in the present moment and take a moment to step back from the experience. Take several deep breaths and step into Awareness. Step BACK and observe! By saying this, I do not mean for you to activate a fight and flight response. I simply mean for you to visualize the experience as if it is playing itself out on a movie screen in front of you and realize this experience is just an illusion, a story that you are playing a part in and so are the others. The confusion or conflict will become clear the moment you become the observer of what is happening, allowing you to actually witness your own developmental programming and how it affects your response as well as the response you get from the others.

When you are observing, be sure to do so from a point of genuine curiosity about yourself and others. Be sure to view all three aspects of the experience: the experience itself, you in the experience, and the processing of the experience, (i.e., how you and the other(s) are responding in the experience). Also determine how that is or is not working. For example, you might say to yourself, "Hey, look at me and look at what I'm doing." And it might be helpful to even say to yourself, "I wonder why I am doing that?" Looking at the others, you might say, "What I just said seems to have triggered them." Or from this place of Awareness you might look at the object of the experience and say, "Well this is not really all that important to me. So, what do I believe about myself that makes me so upset and where did I get this belief from?"

Perhaps you will recognize that the object of the experience is no concern of yours and it's really someone else's issue. Or you may look at how you and the other person are processing the experience and discover that you or the other person are violating a boundary that is important and useful to you or the other person. If this is the case, you might have a need to engage in a conscious dialog where you say your truth about how the experience makes you feel and listen to the other person about how this experience makes them feel. When in dialog with another, it is not helpful to express yourself using "you" statements. For example, "You make me feel," because this causes the other person to become defensive and reactive. It is better to say simply "I" statements like, "I feel this way when that happens."

Journaling

CR: Begin a journal about your experience with Awareness and how you felt from the observer's point of view as you witnessed the experience. Write down what you were able to witness in each aspect of the experience.

Describe the experience itself and what it was about.

Next describe you in the experience, what were you doing?

Did you get triggered by the experience?

How did you react to the trigger?

What if any emotions came up for you?

How did that make you feel?

Do you recognize any of your patterns? If so, what were they?

How did the other(s) react within the experience?

Did they also get triggered?

What might they have been feeling?

What might you have done or said differently if you were given the opportunity to have this same experience again?

Once again, be prepared not to have either all the questions or answers, simply remain open. Allow yourself time to process and allow more questions to come up. It is best to complete the journal entry with a question rather than an answer or a recipe for happiness. This question will then work in the subconscious mind, calling forth answers, intuition, inspiration, and guidance from within.

Connect with Others

CR: Start a conversation with a friend or loved one sharing your experience with Awareness and your insights from your journaling. Do active listening while encouraging the other person to tell their story of an experience they were having and describe how Awareness might work for them. Reflecting with your friend or partner on both stories discuss any missed opportunities or any resistance to stepping into Awareness. Becoming the observer—talk about any feelings or conclusions you had and any needs, attachments, or beliefs you had that might have interfered with using the Awareness process.

Milestones

CR: It takes a lot of practice to step into Awareness quickly when we are triggered and to remain open to intense emotions without acting out our habitual responses of defending our views or territory. Staying open, we can relax in the midst of emotional upheaval and appreciate it for what it is. How we experience this openness depends on how aware we are. After accepting that we have been triggered and opening up to the situation, we learn to discern from the place of Awareness. We find that we can respond with mindfulness versus reacting from habitual patterns and we sharpen our intelligence and become more conscious of what the next best step might be.

Observing our self in the process of Awareness can be irritating and at times disorienting. Anger strikes, our hands are sweaty, our heart beats faster, and our face goes red. However, with the shift to

Awareness, and the practice of mindfulness, we do not judge anything, not ourselves, not the others—we simply observe.

Choose to simply watch, listen, and remain curious instead of blaming and reacting. When dancing with life from the place of Awareness, there is no urge to leave the dance floor. Instead, we remain present with the intensity of the experience along with the triggers, emotions, and patterns. This is even if we wish it were gone and the situation was resolved in some other way. We need to hold a space for our self to complete the experience fully.

When a burst of emotion is expressed habitually, it may result in painful wounds for ourselves and others. Whereas in Awareness, we give some openness and this allows us to recognize the patterns and to use the Life Force Energy that is available to us to transform the experience allowing us to respond in a more harmonious way. Celebrate that you are now able to remain present with the experience and to accept and work with uncertainty, fully attentive to your feelings, the feelings of others, and the experience itself, and sensing what is needed with an open mind and heart. When the mind, body, people, and situations all work together, there is no separation between you, the others, and your individual perceptions. There is simply wholeness and harmony. Celebrate these milestones of processing all your experiences through Awareness. It is a process that leads us to consciously respond and take action from the heart.

Making it Personal

DS: I am a lover of artwork and have learned much from studying great paintings. Masterpiece paintings contain symbolism very useful to life, bring pleasure and joy to the heart, and become incredible guides to different perspectives of life. A great painting will reveal a life span of many years and provide us with the ability to understand our own map of the mind.

During my multiple trips to Rome and Florence, I studied a number of great paintings created by Renaissance's master artists. The Renaissance was a period of light and consciousness that took place between the 14th-16th centuries following the Dark Ages. Renaissance translates as "rebirth" and during that golden period, great contributions were made in art, poetry, paintings, architecture, and philosophy. Renaissance's great artists were totally inspired by the maxim of "Know Thyself" that came out of the heart of the Ancient Greek people.

Art is a powerful way to understand Awareness and indeed the Golden Age of Greece and Renaissance have contributed much to human consciousness. Back in those days, Awareness was recognized as one of the most fundamental values and one's beliefs and virtues were harmonized with their soul. Awareness (know thyself) was to be conscious of your actions and orient your thinking towards the truth, your feelings towards the beautiful, and your actions towards the good.

Strengths and Weaknesses

Awareness is what moves me outside the mind's box and the ability to understand my strengths and weaknesses.

I asked myself the following:

What is my strength towards embracing new possibilities?

What is my weakness when it comes to conflict?

Do I live my life based on what is external to my being or do I live life from what is within me and express my true self to the outside world?

How do I use self-control to avoid being confrontational and avoid projecting my beliefs and perspectives onto others?

There are great benefits from knowing our strengths and our weaknesses. Using Awareness as our way of interpreting and interacting with life, we learn to pay more attention to our feelings, discern our thoughts and emotions, and improve our communication with ourselves and others.

Participant and Observant

Each time I am engaged in a particular experience and I am fully present, interacting with the people and the surroundings witnessing my thoughts and feelings fully, I am a participant in the creation of my life. As a participant, I utilize the existing references of my mind's map.

When I observe an experience and watch it from a distance without any particular attachment to the outcome, and simply accept the experience as it is, I become a direct witness. There is no identification with my thoughts and feelings. I step back from any automatic thinking. I am an observer, gaining access to new ways of seeing and feeling, allowing me more choices and alternative perspectives to the experience.

Three Parts of the Experience

Without a doubt, my early experiences in life have influenced my beliefs and affected the way I live my life. Understanding the map of my mind requires that I expand my Awareness through each one of these experiences. That means to go through all three aspects of an experience. These being: The experience itself; me in the experience; and the processing of the experience.

Paying attention to various experiences and going through the three-part process, just like the one described below, offers a unique opportunity of flushing out automatic reactions and creating better solutions.

Let's Break Down an Experience

I had been working with another family member towards the completion of a great event. We both would be acting as the event's hosts and main speakers. We had set the date, booked the place, and sent out all the invitations. All details were finalized and we were ready to go. However, right at the last minute, and before the event was to take place, my co-partner decided to go away on a personal trip and cancelled without any justifiable excuse. His action triggered a feeling of let down that I felt irritated, upset, and angry. My previous feelings of excitement and joy were now mixed with disappointment that prompted me to look into imposing consequences.

The above described the first stage of my experience—where I am a participant to whatever is happening. I am emotionally engaged in the experience using past thoughts and feelings to define it.

Moving in the second part of the experience required that I become the observer in the experience. The idea is to remain free from any emotional involvement or immersed in any known attachments, needs, or specific outcomes. My natural orientation as an observer was to distance myself from automatic impulses, time bound mechanisms, and limiting beliefs, which were part of my mind's programming.

I took a step back to visualize the experience as if it played itself out on an imaginary movie screen and returned to the planning period, listening to different discussions and interactions between myself and others. I paid attention to my thoughts and perceptions as they came and went through the experience. I made notations of any hard or fixed thoughts and feelings asking myself as to why I was having these thoughts and feelings.

I questioned myself about it and evaluated it during the observant stage. I asked myself the following:

Did I suspend all criticizing?

Was I aware of the nature of the experience?

Did I stay free from unhealthy attachments?

This was the second part of the experience, where I simply observed my experience in order to become aware of my thoughts and actions in a non-reactive way.

The third and final part was processing the experience. I considered the situation from the other person's point of view in order to get a better insight of their feelings and thought process so I could respond in a more appropriate way.

I asked myself the following to better understand myself and the others in the experience:

Did I see anything within my own behavior that may have contributed to mine or the other's reactions to the experience?

What might I have done differently in the experience that may have resulted in a different outcome?

How did the other's behavioral reactions inform me?

Why did they act in a prescribed way?

How were they dealing with the experience differently from me?

How did the other's behavior and decision-making affect me in this experience? Could I simply accept the differences?

Asking the right questions and moving into a place of Awareness brought a compassionate understanding of the situation. This helped me get my mind into a neutral and rather natural state of using a higher form of loving energy and understanding.

Awareness shone its brilliant spotlight on my experiences and gave birth to my purpose and potentiality. Awareness is what allowed me to focus on the bigger picture of life and work towards the creation of a stronger relationship with myself and others.

The Mind is the Map

PART I: THE PROCESS

The Critical Voice ... The Writing on Our Wall

III

IV

Understanding Our Patterns

I

FINDING JOY

The voice of our Ego is a major cause of our suffering. It fights life, rails against it, and is discontent and afraid. It is the voice of the false self not the true self. The thoughts that arise in our mind can cause every negative emotion we experience such as: fear, guilt, anger, jealousy, shame, sadness, resentment, envy, hopelessness, worthlessness, and depression.

PART II:

CULTIVATING THE JOURNEY

"*Our character is basically a composite of our habits.*
Because they are consistent, often unconscious patterns,
they constantly, daily, express our character."

- Stephen Covey

CHAPTER FOUR

THE CRITICAL VOICE...THE WRITING ON OUR WALL

CR: THE MIND is a wonderful tool for thinking, but it has a dark side. One of our most basic characteristics of being human is our inner voice—the mind chatter. It is the Ego having a conversation with itself. This causes us to sometimes make snap judgments based on assumptions. We form impressions of others and of the experiences we are having based on the false data coming from the *writing on our wall*.

Our mind chatter is constantly assessing and evaluating and would have us believe that we and the inner voice are the same and that our goals and intentions are the same as the stuff of the mind. Throughout our day, we have conversations with a variety of other people, like family, friends, and coworkers, but there is one person we speak to more than anyone else and that person is our self. What are you saying about yourself in your own mind? This conversation with self comes from the *writing on our wall*.

The mind chatter pretends to be useful, but it is not useful. The Ego is the aspect of our mind that chats with us as we move about our day. It is the voice in our head. Much of the time, this voice seems like our own voice, and we often express these thoughts as, "I love doing that. I can't wait until tomorrow. I wonder what will happen." At other times, this voice is like the voice of a parent or other authority figure or a friend. It says, "You should try harder. Don't forget to take your vitamins." It may even seem evil or mean. "You never do anything right. You're worthless. You might as well give up."

We tend to take this voice seriously. In fact, most often we believe it, agree with it, and don't question it. We believe it because we are programmed, or wired to believe our own thoughts, regardless of whether they are true and helpful or not. Not only do we believe these thoughts, we believe they are "ours." We identify with them. We think they reflect who we are. It is interesting that we don't tend to question our own thoughts, although we readily question other people's thoughts, especially if those thoughts are different from our own. I believe we find it is easier to look "out there" for our answers and, of course, our EGO loves to defend its position of being right. What I do know is that it is never about what is out there! No one, and no thing, "out there" can cause us to feel anything. That is an inside job. Our emotions come from our thoughts. Our thoughts come from our perceptions, and our perceptions come from our beliefs, which are originating from the *writing on our wall*. If we want to change, we need only discover and transform what is *written on our wall*.

This voice of our Ego is a major cause of our suffering. It fights life, rails against it, and is discontent and afraid. It is the voice of the false self not the true self. The thoughts that arise in our mind can cause every negative emotion we experience such as: fear, guilt, anger, jealousy, shame, sadness, resentment, envy, hopelessness, worthlessness, and depression.

Paying attention to this critical voice is a great place to begin our inner work. If you don't hear a critical voice, you might ask yourself if it is just that you haven't recognized it as a critical voice because you mistake it for the truth, or if you simply make sure you're too busy to hear it. Or your voice might speak to you in another way—perhaps a feeling that serves the same purpose in your physical body. Also, you might experience critical messages as thoughts rather than a voice. The critical voice can be in any one of these forms.

I recall doing a workshop and someone said this about their voice, "I can't hear it, I must be really stupid." Or "I can't hear it. I'm failing again." My reply was, "So, does it perhaps say, 'I'm stupid,' or 'I'm failing again?'" Then I see that twinkle and their eyes light up with comprehension. I can see they got it. We become so used to the critical voice that sometimes we don't even hear what we're saying to ourselves.

If we do not address the critical voice, it can have a huge impact on our lives. For one thing, every thought creates a field of energy. Therefore, the thought that is being expressed by the critical voice has an energy field of its own. At a neuro level, there have been huge shifts in our understanding of the mind. Brain cells act as communities—they link up and work together as networks. The more we think a particular thought, the more these networks build themselves and strengthen. Within one hour, the synaptic connections, the link between the cells by which they communicate can double. One hour of focusing on a particularly negative thought, including a thought expressed by the critical voice, will constantly build its neural muscle.

The good news is that when we don't use a network, it simply withers away. Billions of neurons get busy tearing apart a network that seems no longer needed. We rewire ourselves constantly on the basis of what we pay attention to and when we stop buying into, or focusing on, what the critical voice is saying, and instead focus on more positive thinking, we are creating a more positive outcome. We actually can change the connections in our brains. This is the new science of neuroplasticity.

Psychiatrist and psychoanalyst, Norman Doidge, MD, wrote a fascinating, award-winning book on this topic called *The Brain that Changes Itself*. In it he states, "When I first heard news that the human brain might not be hardwired, I had to investigate and weigh the evidence for myself. These investigations took me far from my consulting room. I began a series of travels, and in the process, I met a band of brilliant scientists, at the frontiers of brain science, who had, in the late 1960s or early 1970s, made a series of unexpected discoveries. They showed that the brain changed its very structure with each different activity it performed, perfecting its circuits so it was better suited to the task at hand. If certain "parts" failed, then other parts could sometimes take over. The machine metaphor of the brain as an organ with specialized parts could not fully account for changes the scientists were seeing. They began to call this fundamental brain property 'neuroplasticity.'

Neuro is for "neuron," the nerve cells in our brains and nervous systems. Plastic is for "changeable, malleable, modifiable." At first, many of the scientists didn't dare use the word "neuroplasticity" in their publications, and their peers belittled them for promoting a fanciful notion. Yet they persisted, slowly overturning the doctrine of the unchanging brain. They showed that children are not always stuck with the mental abilities they are born with—that the damaged brain can often reorganize itself so that when one part fails, another can often substitute. That if brain cells die, they can at times be replaced—that many "circuits" and even basic reflexes that we think are hardwired are not. One of these scientists even showed that thinking, learning, and acting can turn our genes on or off, thus shaping our brain anatomy and our behavior. This was surely one of the most extraordinary discoveries of the twentieth century."

New research from an organization called Heart Math revealed that on average we have ten times as many neuro bundles of information going from our brains to our senses as we do from our senses to our brains. We imagine we see the world as it is, but we don't. We see it as we are. We tell our senses what information we want them to collect. For example, when we stop paying attention to the critical voice saying, "I'm not good enough," we actually change the way our brain sends messages to our senses to look for evidence that confirms that statement. The brain does a template matching of sorts. It consistently defers to the *writing on our wall* and it performs a "cross check" for every single experience. We are receiving so much information at any moment that we cannot possibly process it all. So, our mind looks for templates of the experiences we have already had that can make sense of our current experience and matches it with a template. As a result, we act out the same patterns of behavior we always have.

In terms of our patterns, when we get triggered by an event or experience, we feel an emotion causing us to react with our habitual pattern of responding and it is all because of the *writing on our walls.* All of our experiences and memories are stored in our subconscious mind. Any emotions we had at the time of the event, including any conclusions we came to regarding the experience, are bundled with the stored experience. It is *written on our walls* and our subconscious "knows" how to respond from the messages on the walls. For example, if our subconscious could talk to us, it might say something like, "Oh yeah, it's this again. Been there, done that—we do this when that happens!"

This automatic programming speaks to the nature of our patterns and it also answers the questions, "Why do I do that and why do I keep doing that?" There is no longer any doubt about the strong connection between the *writing on our walls* and the way life shows up for us. *"WE Create Our Own Reality based on the Writing on Our Walls."* This statement should be tattooed on the insides of our eyelids so that we see it every time we blink. Its truth is undeniable, yet so subtle that we tend to ignore it.

The *writing on our walls* is our most prominent advisors and we consult it all day long. There is *writing on our walls* for whatever we do and think. Those words represent the "truth" as we have learned it. We consult those walls for just about everything. Those words tell us about our opportunities as well as our limits and very often they conflict with each other. It represents every experience we have ever had. It contains all of our how to's, our cans and our cant's, as well as our shoulds and our should not's. It contains our musts and our must not's. It contains our version of proper behavior, as well as what we consider right or wrong in this world. It contains our judgments, our successes, and our failures. It's all there—everything we hold to be true—*written on our walls.*

We all have different words on our walls. That's why we appear to have different limits. Our limits are different because the "truths" *written on our wall* are different than the "truths" written on the wall of others. But what if they were not truths at all? What if we were to just pause, to stop and reality test this writing? The truth is they are just guidelines we have adopted for getting through life. Some of them are even childhood survival skills, and many of them are fictions. They are hand-me-down beliefs that were *written on our walls* by others and because of the way our physical mind operates, we have been dutifully obeying them ever since.

We can seldom control what will happen in life, or how others will behave, or even the results of our efforts. But we can choose how to feel, react, and respond towards those events and situations. This is actually the basis of our free will. Imagine that life is a card game and that it deals us at each moment certain cards. That is to a large degree (but not totally) out of our hands. Whatever our experience, we can be in control. It is our response-ability and how we choose to play those cards that is our only freedom. The freedom to choose how we want to perceive, feel, respond, and react towards life situations is in our control.

Many believe that our emotions are actually created by what happens, some external event or experience. But that is simply not true. We ourselves create our emotions and we do this by how we choose to perceive the experience. It is not the events or other's behaviors that cause us to feel certain emotions. Our emotions and reactions are the result of our beliefs and childhood conditioning. We can change our beliefs concerning what is happening by shifting our response and reactions to our heart, where they are aligned to the higher state of unconditional love, for self, and for all others. When we are able to do this, our external reality will reflect our new perceptions, emotions, responses and reactions attracting different events and behaviors that create different experiences for us. Without the old programming, we can live in peace within ourselves and in harmony with others. In the next few chapters, we will discuss how we can change our thoughts and create a new reality—one that supports us on our journey of life.

What we find during our discovery process is often not big trauma, it's often everyday drama. It's about the little things that remind us we are human. We experience stress and emotions and sometimes it's important to look back on things that we might not have deemed as anything important. So often we make mistakes as adults in thinking, "Oh that was nothing. It was quite small and it was a long time ago." It might be a small, everyday experience to an adult, but often it wasn't a small experience to a 3- or 4-year-old and the impact it had at that age is what the discovery process is about. The *writing on our wall* is that of the younger self and, of course, we would judge it differently now as an adult.

I'd like to turn our attention now to the other voice in our mind—the Higher Self. This is the voice that whispers reassurances that everything is fundamentally okay and delivers its message with simplicity and quiet confidence. It is amazing that once we hear it, we know it speaks the truth. The still, small voice within each of us does not try to compete with the mental chatter on the surface of our minds, nor does it attempt to overpower the volume of the raucous world outside. If we want to hear it, no matter what is going on around us, or even inside us, we can always tune in to that soft voice underneath the surrounding noise.

The practice of Awareness partnered with meditation helps us to notice the difference between the critical voice and that of our Higher Self. The voice of our Higher Self is always loving, tender, soft, empowering, and never judgmental or critical—it is the inner voice that gives us the gifts of wisdom. The voice of our Higher Self provides us with the knowledge and reassurance that what's *written on our wall* is not the truth of who we are.

The critical voice may never disappear completely. However, it will become a less frequent companion, more muted, and perhaps even an ally that alerts us if we start to fall back into overly critical thoughts about ourselves. Generally, once we pay more attention to the Higher Self and what it has to say, a powerful sense of calm settles over our entire being, and the critical voice, once so dominant, fades into the background, suddenly seeming to be small and far away. There will come a time, after much practice, that we will live our lives with clarity and discernment from the place of pure Awareness, embracing the voice of our Higher Self, and this voice will be our guide to living our best life simply by following the threads of the wisdom offered us.

*

Going Deeper

CR: The critical voice has a number of upsides. The first of which is that it is actually on our side. Whatever it says to us and however unfriendly it sounds, it is almost certainly trying to help in some way. It is telling us what is *written on our walls* and sometimes even why we adhere to our old patterns of behavior. For example, if it says, "We are not good enough," it is as well for us to know that so we don't make ourselves more vulnerable than we need to be. Or if it says, "You don't belong," it might believe it is keeping you safe by making sure you do not try to be included in a group it thinks might reject you and hurt you. It might be trying to keep you safe by reminding you not to try. So instead of criticizing it back, fighting it, or trying to silence it; we can start by thanking the critical voice for what it has been trying to do for us and use it to help us in a different way.

The following questions are not always easy to answer, and many beginners at this process of self-discovery feel frustrated. My suggestion is to try turning this frustration into genuine curiosity about getting to know yourself and others on a deeper level. Play with the mystery and wonder of all that is and remember this is a process of discovery of self!

Ask yourself these questions:

Do I hear/pay attention to the voice in my head?

How often do I hear the voice in my head?

What is it saying to me? Is it positive or critical?

Are these negative statements? What are they?

Are they positive statements? What are those?

Is what the voice is saying ringing true or false?

Reality test what the voice is saying. What do you think about what it says?

Do you believe in what the voice is saying?

Which statements do you concur with? Which statements do you not concur with?

What emotions come up for you when you hear the voice in your head?

Does it sound like someone you might have heard before—perhaps a caregiver?

How does what it says make you feel? Name the emotions.

Journaling

CR: Begin a journal about your experience with the voice in your head. Reality test what the voice says and to capture the details it says and record it. Go ahead and respond to the voice and tell the voice how you feel, as in both emotions and your reactions. Use this journal entry as a running journal—a tool to record everything the voice says to you. What the voice is saying is a good indicator of the *writing on your wall.* We want to know in our discovery process what is *written on the wall* and remember this writing is not who you are—it's someone else's story! Make notes of any disagreements or conflicts you feel with what the voice has to say.

Once again, be prepared not to have either all the questions or answers—remain open. Rather than try to solve all the problems, allow time to process and allow more questions to come up. Remember that it is often best to complete the journal entry with a question rather than an answer.

Connect with Others

CR: Start a conversation with a friend or loved one sharing your experience with the voice in your head and your insights from your journaling. Do active listening while encouraging the other person to tell their story of how the voice in their head shows up for them. Reflecting with your friend or partner on both the experiences and the stories, discuss any conflicts or reactions either of you had to what the voice said. Discuss any missed opportunities to feeling things fully and how any needs, attachments, or beliefs you might have had that interfered with or even supported the voice.

Milestones

CR: Most of us have a very limited "intimate" contact with the voice in our head. By ignoring it and maintaining our habitual patterns, we are deadening ourselves to our inner world. An honest examination of these recurring conversations and the patterns or the way they make us feel—the way we react to our emotions—the way we think in terms of rigid belief systems—is the way to quiet the mind. By becoming intimate with our inner voice, we can learn a lot about our self.

Through the practice of monitoring the inner voice we learn to recognize and experience ourselves more directly, coming to know more and more intimately why we do what we do or think what we think. Be sure to celebrate the courage and honesty required to look at what lies underneath what the voice is saying and witness the discovery of how your thoughts continuously create your reality. Celebrate your ability to constantly create change and dismantle the critical voice as you learn to experience what's *written on your walls* in a gentle, loving way.

Making it Personal

DS: Like the outer world, our inner world is complex and has the capacity to handle myriads of thoughts, memories, and feelings about these thoughts and memories. Our inner world is a mixture of conscious, subconscious, and unconscious thoughts and beliefs all synthesized to create our outer world. Within this network each and every word and feeling has its own energy, and no matter how tiny each of our thoughts or feelings are, they will affect our life.

Our mind works in a fascinating way and uses the brain's hundreds of billions of nerve cells at incredible speeds to process images, thoughts and feelings, and communicates to us the messages *written on our walls.*

Our perceptions of reality become the sum of these internal concepts that shape our decisions.

What we believe creates our reality and just like Gandhi says, "Our beliefs become our thoughts, our thoughts become our words, our words become actions, our actions become habits, our habits become our values and our values become our destiny."

Our mind is programmed to work like a computer that processes information with an input and an output that spits out results. The difference is that when working with a computer, when we see something that we don't like, all we have to do is delete it. However, it is not so easy with our mind. We tend to identify with our inner voice and the thoughts, memories, and beliefs *written on our walls*. Once this happens, our thought process becomes repetitious and ceaseless. Our unconscious level is like an unfathomable ocean carrying the memories of our entire life and uses our inner voice as a surfing board to reach the shore of the conscious mind.

A good number of our thoughts and beliefs are not within our Awareness. We keep looking at our world through the filtered lens of our own unique perspectives and make assumptions that limit our choices.

Although we don't have the power to control the outside world, we can monitor and transform our own thoughts and emotions. We start by realizing that our inner voice and our inner critics are like utility poles, conduits of fusion of concepts, thoughts, beliefs, patterns and behaviors coming from the subconscious and unconscious levels of our mind.

Our inner and critical voice simply propels the existence of past memories and/or any future anxiety we may have. Some of them are good and others not so pleasant and the energy of these are manifested through our body sensations.

On the Journey of Self Discovery

Once we begin the journey of self-discovery, we never turn back. We cannot "unknow" something we have discovered. We embark on a mission to find our authentic self and create a new map of our mind. The previous programming of the mind becomes obsolete and soon we begin to open the door to our destiny.

One of the first things that I asked myself was what defines me and who am I?

Was I the sum of previous beliefs, conclusions, and a reflection of my needs, wants, and reactions? Or do I have a different purpose in life?

Was I the image of a personality developed over the years through a web of old beliefs, thoughts, and emotions stored in a memory bank or a universal creation of new ideas, hopes, and dreams?

While observing my behaviors, I realized that certain habitual patterns were undermining my happiness. Over the years I had developed a high expectancy for acceptance and respect. I needed to be valued and liked by others and when those desires were not met, I would feel disappointed.

I listed a number of my positive and negative habitual patterns that would help me identify how I was relating to the outside world and how I kept defining my own reality.

What were my responses to expectations such as acceptance, respect, and my need to be valued?

What beliefs did I have that were behind these automated patterns?

How flexible was I towards changing my current habitual patterns, inner thoughts, and beliefs?

Unbundling the existing template of my mind required full cooperation with my inner critic. By engaging in a constructive dialogue,

I was able to identify a number of disharmonies and became aware of my automated reactionary programs that kept skipping my Awareness.

Through a number of provoking questions, I engaged my inner critic and became an observer. These questions included:

What were my inner critic's daily habits and thoughts during the morning, afternoon, and evening?

What kind of thoughts lowered my energy and kept limiting me? How did each thought affect the different areas of my life?

Why did my thoughts keep repeating themselves?

How could I undo the programming of my internalized beliefs, behaviors, and memories of past experiences stored in my memory bank?

Changing our thoughts changes the reality of our life, giving it new meaning and increasing our potential in many areas.

Mind Chattering

Mind chattering is made up of past conditioning. It is the voice of our history—a barrage of uninterrupted thoughts based on our beliefs. Mine, just like yours, is unique and keeps reflecting on the past and projects into the future.

It starts early in the morning. As soon as I open my eyes, I am jammed with a number of unplanned thoughts and this same pattern repeats itself several times during the day.

Observation and careful documentation provided me with a list of the inner critics subtle and misleading chattering of thoughts. A few of these include:

A. Self-judging of my decisions and prejudging others

B. Doubting myself and others

C. Blaming and complaining

D. Jumping from likes to dislikes

E. Repeating things over and over again

F. Becoming overwhelmed with issues

G. Displaying a degree of deprivation, incompleteness, and fearfulness

This led me to ask myself the following:

"What is the purpose of the mind chattering?

Is it rational?

How do I work to ease its activity?"

The Inner Critic and Judging

While most of the time we don't understand much about ourselves, we self-judge and criticize others. We believe that there is something wrong with the other person or the world around us without realizing that all is within us. By having such negative thoughts, we keep adding more stress in our life.

One of the main points to address is to identify what your inner critic is saying and to reality test it by asking yourself if you agree with the message.

So, the next thing I did was to question if my inner critic's blaming was true, useful, and did it serve any good purpose?

What did I believe about the other person, or the world, that caused me to be judgmental?

What was my past history of judging and its purpose?

What were the limitations of judging myself and others?

What was the nature of those old beliefs?

How much attention was I paying to the external world versus the internal world?

Judgment can be replaced with wonder leaving open the portal to the heart and it can create a new window of discovery. Furthermore, if our intention is to live a happy life, we must stop taking our inner critic too seriously and stop judging ourselves and others.

The Inner Critic and the "Fight or Flight" Response

Most of us are familiar with the fight or flight response as a way of dealing with a threatening situation or moving away from something stressful. While this approach has served us well in the past, such as when we were running into the caves or climbing up trees to survive, it can no longer serve us and will keep limiting our life. When our mind uses this involuntary approach as a means of protection, we need to question ourselves as to what is perceived as a threat. Is it something real or just in our imagination?

While dealing with a challenging situation, we need to be aware of what is going on inside our head. What is our inner critic's connection to fear and doubt that creates these uncertainties?

Is what we perceive true or a distortion of our thoughts?

We keep searching to find out the ways in which our inner critic is sabotaging our happiness and robbing us out of the present moment.

I found the following questions very useful:

In what ways does my inner critic keep following the same thoughts and patterns from the subconscious and unconscious levels?

What kind of language does my inner critic use when influenced by the emotion of fear or doubt?

How is fear operating in my body and my life?

Which of my childhood wounds continue to impact my life making me feel unsafe?

How does my inner critic interpret various situations? Are these situations really threatening or just a mental creation?

How could I create a complete inner sense of self-control and overcome the "fight or flight" approach and heighten my sense of Awareness?

Fear impacts many areas of our life. Our inner critic tends to act like a preset alarm that keeps ringing to false urgencies creating doubt and ambiguity without any real need. Wholeness is living our life as our own Chief Commander of the mind moving away from the inner critical voices that keep limiting our joy and happiness.

Shifting from the Inner Critic to the I AM

The wisdom tribute, "Know thyself…" Holy is that space, requires that we examine our current life, check our limited beliefs, and develop the willingness of rebirth to our higher human self.

Self-observation and journaling allowed me to create an in-depth evaluation and relieved my mind from its continuous programming. Part of my self-realization process was to transform the previous structure of my mind by taking charge of my thoughts and allowing them to flow through the golden light of my heart.

I was glad to discover that over time the voice of the inner critic subsided and softened while my new intimate relationship with myself led me to a true connection with my Higher Self and the discovery of my own perfect nature, my I am.

Our I am, Ego Eimi, is our higher consciousness and represents our perfect humanness. Our I am is always alive within us, a constant luminous experience of our completeness and wholeness.

The Mind is the Map

PART I: THE PROCESS

Emotional
Intelligence

III   IV
V

Understanding
Our
Patterns

**FINDING
JOY**

Cultivating Emotional Intelligence is one
of the most powerful ways to transform
our life and become consciously aware of
our beliefs and feelings. It helps us create
positive change and improve the quality
of our relationships. These changes will lead
to higher levels of conscious engagement
with our families, friends, and colleagues.

"Emotional Intelligence is the ability to sense, understand, and effectively apply the power and acumen of emotions as a source of human energy, information, connection, and influence."

- Robert K. Cooper. Ph.D.

CHAPTER FIVE

EMOTIONAL INTELLIGENCE

C R: WE ARE dealing with people's emotions all the time and often we are not even aware of this. But how do we recognize their emotions so automatically? Our general intelligence is the brain power that fuels logic, puzzles, and math problems. It also has an emotional counterpart, which researchers have named Emotional Intelligence.

Emotional Intelligence is feeling, knowing, and understanding our emotions and using wisdom and discernment to help us avoid the misunderstandings that lead to anxiety. We seem to need it more than ever in these challenging and testing times. Awareness isn't enough—and it's not enough to be intelligent—we need to use our Awareness, partnered with Emotional Intelligence for the best outcome.

People with high Emotional Intelligence generally find that they have an extra dose of curiosity, which adds to improved responsiveness, increases in their quality of life, a rise in effectiveness, and helps in decision making. It's like a muscle and a skillset that can be learned and strengthened. They are self-aware, self-managing, and self-directing. They do more than just engage in introspection or try to understand their behavior and reactions to their experiences in life. Through the practice of self-awareness, they enact their willpower to change negative behaviors to self-manage their lives in ways that create inner peace. By using their willpower, they are able to self-direct their lives with appropriate responses in all their experiences and to the people they're interacting with.

People with higher Emotional Intelligence are active listeners. They show up, hold a space for others to express themselves, and they are always fully engaged in the present moment. They have the ability to remain present in Awareness of their circumstances, and through this self-awareness, self-realization, self-managing, and self-direction, they are able to transform their experiences into something meaningful for self and for others. They understand that our individual realities are created by our thoughts—knowing that happiness and despair come from within and not from any external sources. Some of the experiences we perceive as unexpected surprises please us, whereas situations we perceive to be not conducive to success or unpromising, can cause us no end of grief.

As we stated earlier, life can seem to be unpredictable and we as humans, tend to focus on the negative experiences, assuming the positive ones will take care of themselves. Life is no more or no less what we think it is and if we look at all the things we have accomplished, and make each new situation our own, the world will become a much brighter place. A simple change in attitude and a shift to Awareness can help us evaluate our potential for fulfillment in every perceived positive experience and every perceived setback.

Living a life with Emotional Intelligence is a process of re-learning how to view life's complexities as though the experience itself is on a movie screen and we are the observer standing in Awareness watching all the aspects of the experience. As the observer, we are witnessing our own involvement in the experience; the others within the experience; and the processing of the experience. And as we have discussed in a previous chapter, these are the three aspects to every experience. While in Awareness, we must try to rid ourselves of any preconceived ideas of what is good and what is bad so that we can appreciate the rich insights hiding within the experience.

Using our Emotional Intelligence, we can imagine ourselves as surfers riding incoming waves of information and inspiration, always open and willing to attune ourselves to the current experience. We will see how fortunate we are to have these opportunities to play on the waves and, most of all, to enjoy the ride whilst we are learning and growing. We are not victims of our circumstances—we simply take on roles that we think are tolerable or expected of us. Some people are working in professions, careers, and even their own businesses that they really didn't consciously plan to pursue and don't really like. Many others feel they are in relationships where they are not truly happy. Understand that it is our thoughts that create our feelings and if not kept in check, our reality will become filled with dysfunctional thoughts, feelings, or beliefs.

We can cultivate Emotional Intelligence through the Awareness and the discovery processes and we are able to transform thoughts, beliefs, and feelings that were once misinformed thoughts or dysfunctional behaviors into thoughts that serve us better and are in perfect symmetry and order. As we transform our thoughts, we transform our feelings and transform our life, and even the lives of those around us.

In the self-discovery process, remain in a state of Awareness, witnessing the events unfold in a state of curiosity, simply enjoy the wonder of the process and let go of any pre-conceived outcomes. Pay particular attention to the cause and effects of the thinking mind and how these affect the way life is showing up for you. What we will experience is an opening in our hearts beyond anything we have imagined. We will discover how to increase our love and appreciation for every aspect of life, while receiving profound insights on how we can create more fulfilling and caring relationships. We re-awaken our birthright as a true genius, transcending any fears and illusions sur-rounding the stories we have been telling ourselves and we are able to reconnect with our true mission and purpose for life.

It has been said that there is a gift in every experience. While in the witness state observing our circumstances or experiences, one aspect of the self-awareness process is to become curious enough to find the gift of the experience. Nothing has ever happened or will happen to us that is not a gift and a blessing. However, it's difficult to be thankful until we find the hidden benefit in what may seem at first to be a negative experience. Even what we might perceive as the most terrible experi-ence or event will always contain hidden blessings. It is helpful to also understand that what we perceive as blessings can also trigger a crisis. Stepping into Awareness, we are less likely to be upset about difficul-ties we encounter in our life. That is one of the secrets of Emotional Intelligence. In other words, balance is neither pessimism nor opti-mism. It is gratefulness and that is both wisdom and true power. It is in becoming the witness through Awareness of what it is that we are able to remain centered no matter what happens around us.

Cultivating Emotional Intelligence is one of the most powerful ways to transform our life, become consciously aware of our beliefs, and feelings about our self. Developing our Emotional Intelligence helps us create positive change in our personal lives and helps us improve the quality of our relationships with others. These changes will lead to higher levels of conscious engagement with our families, friends, and colleagues. As we integrate this higher level of Emotional Intelligence into our way of being in and of this world, it will expand further, perhaps creating improved social Emotional Intelligence in our schools, our communities, and even our countries and will contribute to a deeper understanding between nations improving the world around us.

The mind is the greatest gift. It is the map to understanding our self. Awareness is the compass to higher levels of consciousness that leads us to live from our heart. Through our understanding of the mechanisms and workings of the mind, we can see that using our Emotional Intelligence guides us to connecting with our heart, to living from the heart, to living the divine essence of pure unconditional love. There is nothing more magnificent than the human body, brain, and spirit working in unison.

We can practice Emotional Intelligence and live the story being told to us by our intuitive spirit, the story linked to our destiny. It is the action of processing our thinking of the mind through Awareness of the self and reacting mindfully from the heart. This is the great leap in consciousness, moving from the thinking mind into the knowing heart. By cultivating the practice of Emotional Intelligence, we are able to see the underlying patterns and perfect order of the Universe, experiencing an illuminating state of gratitude.

DS: Christina, you are right. Awareness is not enough. We need Emotional Intelligence as well. During the course of my life, I have met many intelligent and successful people, but their brilliance was more self-serving than serving others. Their level of Emotional Intelligence showed very little understanding of other people's feelings.

There are also many emotionally intelligent people who identify with and manage their own emotions and who have tremendous empathy towards the emotions of others. The hearts of these wonderful human beings are constantly filled with humility and love and show their great manners towards others.

I remember you once said, "Every event, every outcome is an expression of love from the Universe—giving us the opportunity to realize the truth or not. We all have free will."

Indeed, free will is a force within us that creates movement and allows us to become present to the unfolding of our inner experiences. Will is what causes our movement and our ability to transform our emotions into positive thoughts that serve us well. Our willpower is like a muscle that is either well-built or frail. Discipline strengthens our will and makes us able to endure life's burdens by remaining steadfast to challenges. Author James N Watkins once introduced us to an inspirational quote, "A river will cut through a rock not because of power but because of its persistence." Our will works in the same way. Persistence in using our will gives us the ability to exercise strength. Our outside victories are determined by winning the inner battles and we increase our ability to balance our emotions with positive thoughts by using our inner will.

We experience our will like air in our lungs. We breathe without thinking and we provide energy to every cell of our body. By becoming conscious of the enormous power of our will, we witness the reasons why we act or react in one way or another and we begin to discover our true purpose in life.

We all have the willpower to touch the sky, the Universe, the hand of God. Our willpower brings us to natural truths and gives rise to our intentions. Simply remember the magic words, I can and I will.

It is important to understand that from all the works of God we are the brightest, the purest, and a true universal gift of beauty. Each of us has developed spiritual eyes that enable us to see remarkable light aspects of the world. Our mind is one of the greatest gifts and the space of creation of all our great thoughts. Using our imagination and Emotional Intelligence, we can envision the glorious and divine spiritual beauty of life and divinity.

Going Deeper

CR: While a generalized approach will reduce complexity—and it may work well for some people—optimal learning is personal. When it comes to a single person, we're all different, unique human beings, and whatever worked for you, might not work for others. One commonality is that far too often we overreact with too much emotion, or we underreact with too little emotion. Living with Emotional Intelligence is a step forward in learning to lead and live from the heart embracing our own feelings as a source of insight, welcoming and embracing our feelings, even the complicated ones, as a way to understand what's going on for us and for the others in our experiences. It's easy when the feelings are what we want. But the best learning is when we are willing to be courageous and open enough to engage with our emotions even when they're difficult.

Emotional Intelligence is an "inside job" that begins with the foundation of an enhanced self-discovery into your unique patterns of behavior that then fuels your choices with the goal of supporting your values and purpose in living. Turn inward, be curious about who you really are, and then show up to support the change you wish to be in the world. Be comfortable with your emotions, especially because emotions have functions. Emotions are not just about feeling something. You want to determine, "What's the message of the emotion?"

Self-reflection is another step towards practicing Emotional Intelligence. Try to sit silently for a few minutes every day and practice self-introspection. Create, remember, and become aware of your own tales, your stories are linked with particular experiences, moods, feelings and emotional states. Notice the blends of emotions in your stories. You may experience many emotions at once. Try to identify all your emotions. When you want to change your feelings, remember the stories, and the range of feelings that emerge.

Here are some tips to assist you to put your Emotional Intelligence into action:

- Be an observer of yourself. Pay attention to what you feel and how those feelings contribute, distract, enhance, or challenge you. Awareness is the first step.
- Starting with self-awareness—acknowledge your emotions and where you feel them in your body.
- Become more emotionally literate. Build your emotional vocabulary. Be able to name your emotions.
- Train yourself to sense your emotions via sensations in your body.
- While in Awareness, try to acknowledge your emotions. Think of them not as good or bad, right or wrong, but as a source of information that helps you gain self-awareness.
- Become an expert at unpacking your emotions and thinking. This is about stopping and asking, "Wait a minute—what's going on for me here? What am I feeling? What am I thinking? And what does all this mean for me?"
- Notice your own strengths and lean into your strengths more fully.
- Pay attention to the thoughts and feelings in the present moment. Do this with purpose, non-judgmentally, and do this as if your life depended on it.
- Step into Awareness and recognize your patterns. Notice when you set yourself up for low Emotional Intelligence moments that become patterned habitual habits. Be aware of two common traps, which are:
  1. Passing critical judgment on others only serves to elevate or affirm one's superiority over another person's choices, or intelligence. Emotional Intelligence begins when we learn to recognize these habitual patterns and then retrain

ourselves to restrain from making any negative comment at all.

2. Taking offense is another part of recognizing patterns and it is a struggle for many of us. In today's world, we have been taught to take offense at even the most trivial matters. Taking offense and feeling offended, can quickly escalate to criticism, judgment, bitterness, and lack of forgiveness to pain. This affects our relationships and even our own health. You are practicing Emotional Intelligence when you notice the other person's comment or action, and instead of taking offense and taking it personally, just consider it as data. Remain the observer only!

Another thing we can do when we find ourselves reacting to a situation is to try to determine if any of our core values or personal boundaries are being challenged and, thus, resulting in our unconscious emotional response. This allows us to dive straight to the heart of why a situation is affecting us and begins to shift us out of our habitual reaction and into a more considered response.

There's a lot of discussion on the importance of focusing on strengths instead of weaknesses. For example: Does Emotional Intelligence work best when we choose to focus on our weaknesses or when we leverage our strengths? In my experience, the answer is somewhere in the middle. The fact is something within us needs to be discovered or uncovered and that "something" needs our attention. It is through our self-discovery process where we are challenged to see, accept, and break our habitual patterns. Looking at our full range of needs, attachments, and our capabilities can assist us with the learning process.

Consider the following questions:

When does the most effective learning take place for you?

What data are you able to discover that informs you about your emotions?

What data are you able to discover related to your needs and attachments?

What does it mean to you to live from the Heart?

Where might you focus your attention for growth?

Journaling

CR: When engaging in anything new, and especially if it involves change, you will want to increase your Life Force Energy. I like to use what I call "*golden nuggets*" that we all have. Think about a time in your life when your Life Force Energy was at an all-time high for you. Revisit that experience. Feel your energy increasing. This is one of your golden nuggets. Write about this in as much detail as you can.

This past golden nugget is one that you can use to motivate you when times get tough? Read it often!

Write of a past success and include any acts of Emotional Intelligence you used to help you achieve your goal.

Know that there are five elements we might consider when working with cultivating our Emotional Intelligence. They are all related to trust. In relation to Emotional Intelligence, spend time pondering them and be sure to ask yourself what they mean to you and include these in your writing. These elements are: Commitment, Consistency, Care, Competence, and Communication.

Connect with Others

CR: Start a conversation with a friend or loved one sharing your experience and your insights from your journaling. Emotional Intelligence is one of the most powerful learning solutions and it is unique and meaningful to the one learning. Remember, we all see things from our own unique perspective. When engaging with others keep your heart and mind open—holding a space to listen to what the others have to say. Remember that, "No Way is The Way." The most powerful growth comes from an approach that's uniquely you. One-size fits none.

Milestones

CR: Learning Emotional Intelligence is like training and fine-tuning muscles that may not have been used. The elation we feel when we have learned an important lesson, achieved a goal, or had a big breakthrough can sometimes be met with a period of downtime afterwards. During this period of transition, we may feel unsure and not know where to turn next. Many people, during the pause between achievements, begin to wonder what their life is about. These feelings are common and strike everyone from time to time. Human beings are active creatures; we feel best when we are working on a project or vigorously pursuing a goal. But there is nothing inherently wrong with spending a day, a week, or even a month, simply existing and not having a plan. Just be. It won't be long before you embark upon your next voyage of growth and discovery.

Celebrate your successes. Honoring yourself in this way is a motivator for achieving higher levels of success. As you think clearly about issues that require reflection, you will find that you are strengthening your Emotional Intelligence's muscles. Your mind is getting sharper and you will begin to cultivate your intuition to reach higher levels of truth and knowing. This higher knowledge will enable you to see a bigger picture and a solution. Practice Emotional Intelligence in any situation, any experience, or any problem you face.

Making it Personal

DS: Throughout my life I have been blessed with many of what I call my Golden Nuggets.

My first three golden nuggets in my life were empathy, compassion, and appreciation for others. I was always driven by my good instincts and my desire to communicate well and understand people's feelings. I have been blessed with a gift of empathy passed down to me from my affectionate and lovely mother. She taught me how to have compassion and how to live in the moment with joy and appreciation for others. I learned to praise them for their efforts while helping them overcome life's difficulties. Using the compassion, I learned from my Mom, I was able to tune in to the needs of others recognizing and experiencing the softness of their hearts.

Happiness at Work

I graduated from college at the age of 27 and within a year, I started my own business. I was always enthusiastic about the type of work I was involved with. My passion for success took me through different pathways. I always had the energy, desire, and courage needed to push forward.

For over 30 years, I worked hard to build a good business, establish good relationships with clients, set new systems in place, and hired skillful and loyal employees towards the creation of a strong and productive company. I was loving what I was doing and putting my whole heart into it. Over these years, I was fortunate enough to enjoy a continuous growth of the business and life kept blessing me with a number of successes.

Sometimes our leadership roles will increase the level of our stress. The question becomes how much stress can one tolerate? After 30 years, the complexity of issues, along with the obstacles and the uncertainty increased the levels of my stress and began to chip away my enjoyment of the business. Simply enough, I did not have the tools to deal with the ongoing pressures. At times I found myself engaged in negative self-talk and often overacting to circumstances.

I felt that the time had come to make a choice between earning more money and being happy. I was consistently dealing with the ups and downs of the business, navigating my own emotions and the emotions of others, and at the same time, wrestling with my own tolerance for stress.

Awareness of this new reality guided me onto the path of self-discovery as a way of self-assessment. My wish was to learn more about Emotional Intelligence as a way to understand my own emotions and the emotions of others. I wanted to understand how external triggers work and to realize my inner and outer power.

I took the time and effort to reflect on issues using techniques and practices of self-awareness, self-discovery, and self-realization. And while I was going through the different processes, my heart's courage and determination was embracing new perspectives and a host of new possibilities towards the way I perceived my work environment.

I knew that I deserved happiness and inner peace in my work environment and so did the others who worked there. This made me wonder as to how I could create a truly remarkable workplace for everyone.

Reducing stress and overcoming the emotions causing anxiety in a busy and challenging environment is not easy and navigating ours and other's emotions requires Emotional Intelligence.

I asked myself the following:

How could I use Emotional Intelligence to remove the barriers of separation and create a happy working environment?

How could I understand my own emotions and the emotions of others?

How could I handle conflict in an easier and less stressful way?

What would it take to eliminate blaming and transform any negative energy within the work place?

How could I encourage and engage myself and others to nurture great working relationships and provide a network of inner support?

How could I promote a social workplace for expanding ideas and creativity?

Like Christina has said, "The truth is that lasting happiness will be achieved only when the mind itself has let go of its need to find external sources of happiness. Many of our thoughts and emotions block our happiness and the reason is that our mind has been programmed to seek happiness from external sources. We must learn to reverse this process by asking the right questions and we will discover that our happiness is within us."

Our purpose in life is to find happiness and make the best of our life.

Mastering the art of happiness requires laughter as beauty's remedy. Smiling has helped me go through tough events and uncomfortable thoughts, lifting up my moods and decreasing my stress.

My fourth golden nugget has been the art of happiness.

Security

"Security is mostly a superstition. It does not exist in nature, nor do the children of men as a whole experience it. Avoiding danger is no safer

in the long run than outright exposure. Life is
either a daring adventure, or nothing."

- Helen Keller

Life is eternally flowing, a series of unplanned events, challenges, and excitement and while the outcome of many events turns in our favor, there are others that don't unfold as we expected.

Over the years I faced many challenges head on and I had to deal with a number of obstacles. Courage became my capacity of going beyond the ordinary sense of the world and finding orientation in the absence of familiar benchmarks. However, the uncertainty of some challenging situations delegated a number of security barriers for me and this kept preventing me from living free and fulfilled. At times I was acting like an oyster that felt the need to close to protect its pearl.

The practice of Emotional Intelligence allowed me to accomplish a positive change. First it was by embracing uncertainty and then by engaging with a number of difficult emotions.

I asked myself the following:

What was I thinking and feeling when the issue of insecurity came up?

How could I use this uncertainty as a guide to my future?

What were the patterns of my security barriers and what were the illusionary thoughts that shadow the possibility of clear thinking?

How much was I willing to let go of in the way of outside securities?

How could I listen and trust my inner guidance more closely?"

Outside security is only a superstition. We must develop the willingness to let go of anything outside of ourselves to feel secure. First, we need to break down the emotional prison walls and allow our heart's courage and determination to embrace all possibilities and this will open the door to our destiny.

Through the processes of discovery and the practice of Emotional Intelligence, I realized that what I perceived as external security did not exist. Instead, it was inner security that made me feel protected. It was my own inner security that was going to give me a sense of well-being.

Inner security became my fifth golden nugget in life.

Self Esteem, Net Worth, Self-Worth

*"You can be the most beautiful person in the world
and everybody sees light and rainbows when they
look at you, but if you yourself don't know it, all of
that doesn't even matter. Every second that you spend
on doubting your worth, every moment that you use
to criticize yourself, is a second of your life wasted,
is a moment of your life thrown away. It's not like
you have forever, so don't waste any of your seconds,
don't throw even one of your moments away."*

- C. Joy Bell C.

Through my experiences of running an organization for many years, I can say that the business choices I made were serving the pathway to my destiny more than the balance sheet. But still my inner critic kept judging me about certain decisions creating uncomfortable feelings, comparing me to others, perhaps in an attempt to equate my self-worth to net worth. Also, my personas brought to light their unique insecurities, often in frequently outbursts of their limited beliefs. Of course, this was the *writing on my wall.*

My inner critic kept using my net worth to judge my self-worth. The barrage of questions went something like this:

Where was I standing in regards to others in similar fields?

Was I making enough money?

Did I have enough power?

Was I surrounded with strong people?

Had I achieved much over these years?

This kind of self-judgment was not only divisive, but it kept me from experiencing happiness and fulfillment. It made me realize that it's easy to allow outside events, challenges and circumstances to sabotage your self-esteem and self-worth. This is especially true in a business environment where the mind is programmed to society's pitch and promotion of self-importance. All of this leads up to a complete loss of the authentic self.

Furthermore, my personal discovery process, and the practice of Emotional Intelligence, made me aware of all the energy of certain emotions, especially those that were negating my self-worth.

Once again, I questioned myself:

How did I define my self-worth?

What did it consist of? What did I feel added to or depleted my self-worth?

What did I believe about myself or anything external that was causing me to compare my self-worth to my net worth?

How was my self-esteem defining my self-worth? What heightened my self-esteem and what negated it?

What did I believe about myself or anything external that my self-worth was based on?

How was I experiencing my own self-worth and what was its true value based on for me?

In what ways did the business environment and society influence my self-worth?

What might I believe about myself that caused me to continue feeling insecure and what were the triggers that caused me to act out my beliefs?

In what ways did my beliefs distort my perception of reality?

Often our journey in life requires seeking the advice and wisdom of others. In this case, I asked the advice of my friend, Christina, the co-author of this book. Her words of wisdom resonated very well in my mind.

She stated, "ALL and everything is within your inner beauty since everything that the UNIVERSE is, is also in you. When you know your self-worth and SEE it, you can fight for all that is deserved, no matter how difficult or challenging it may seem to others. Just do it!

Don't put on a disguise or change for other people's satisfaction or desires and do not give permission to anyone to rule your kingdom. Being the only Ruler of the planet LOVE—you are priceless having within you the planets of beauty, strength, emotions, righteousness, and more."

Taking Christina's advice to heart helped me to overcome a great deal of the mind's programming and my inner critic's evaluation of my self-worth. Just like a good conductor that pays attention to the notes being played, I started to pay attention to my thoughts and emotions. No longer was there the need for any external benchmark or measuring tape to determine my self-worth. My self-worth was a product of how much I was truly loving myself. This became my sixth golden nugget in life.

Emotional Intelligence and the Heart

Imagine being a conductor of an orchestra, having the skills, talents and understanding of musical notes. After mastering the art of listening to musical organs and their rhythmical flow, you efficiently communicate the melodic notes to musicians and audiences bringing harmonious music to all.

Emotional Intelligence works in a similar way. But instead of working with musical notes, you work with your emotions and the emotions of others being aware of the power, energy, and sensitivity of each word. After uniting your soul's capacities of feelings, thinking, and willing you begin seek the intention and joy for yourself and others.

Our heart is the center of our feelings, our compass of life, and the direction of our spiritual existence. While our mind recognizes things such as internal images and reflects on our previous experiences, it is our heart that provides the necessary warmth and light towards feeling these images.

My desire was to learn how to shift my thoughts into deeper levels of my heart and to balance my thoughts from the statistical and factual mind with those of the cosmic and universal heart.

I asked myself the following:

What do I need to do to overcome the mind conditioning?

How could the Life Force Energy allow me to flow my thoughts into the region of the cosmic heart?

We need to remember that our heart has all the beauty and warmth; its interiority resonates with all that exists. Our heart can accommodate heaven and earth and will bring unity and balance to our lives including our work environment.

In today's world, we seldom control what will happen on the outside. But we can choose how to feel and learn to use Emotional Intelligence to balance our emotions with pure thoughts and be blessed with God's oneness and bring peace and unity to our world.

We must realize that it is our heart that embodies the true essence of our life and it offers beauty, warmth, and sacred capabilities maintaining all relationships between our cells, organs, brain, body, and the world. Our mind thinks while our heart feels and in cooperation, love's transcendent power raises our soul to a level of divine consciousness.

Our mind is the King and our heart the Queen and when they work together as one, we can live a life with unity, in rhythm and balance with the Universal energy that fills our world with unconditional love. Keep embracing all of life's experiences and the magic of life will begin to reveal itself. Life is a gift and a loan from God. Be ready—we will face our greatest opposition when we are closest to our biggest miracle.

Cultivating Emotional Intelligence through the ardor of the heart is my seventh golden nugget in life.

The Mind is the Map

PART I: THE PROCESS

VI — The Mind is Not Free to be Happy

FINDING JOY

The only difference between our happiness and our suffering is not the way things are in the moment, it's our responses to them. It's our acceptance or rejection and these moments cannot be anything other than what they are. Wishing things were different does absolutely nothing but make us suffer and cause undue unhappiness. Fortunately, you can control your moments.

PART II: CULTIVATING THE JOURNEY

EUDAIMONIA

happiness according to the greeks

EUDAIMONIA (n) lit "human flourishing" a state of being happy, healthy and prosperous.

"The fountain of contentment must spring up in the mind. They who have so little knowledge of human nature as to seek happiness by changing anything but their own dispositions will waste their lives in fruitless efforts and multiply the grief which they purpose to remove."

- Samuel Johnson

CHAPTER SIX

THE MIND IS NOT FREE TO BE HAPPY

CR: ON A "happiness quest," people often reject difficult feelings—and even blame themselves for feeling something "less" than bliss. Here is just one example: "I SHOULD be blissfully happy, but I'm not." That mismatched thought, between expectation and reality, is one of the main causes of unhappiness. In fact, sometimes we increase our unhappiness by rejecting our own real, useful feelings of worry and discontent, attempting to replace "real" with "pleasant."

I suspect that many of us fall into this trap—we're "supposed to be happy," and in trying to be so, we push aside feelings that seem contrary to bliss. We suppress the uncomfortable feelings, thinking that will make room for happiness. But when we suppress any feeling, we suppress all feelings. Instead of increasing happiness by rejecting those "negative" feelings, we just create numbness.

It is this emotional favoritism that makes it extremely difficult to move forward. Emotions serve to signal opportunity and threat, and at the core, they are necessary to alert us and we use this emotional data to solve emotional problems. For example, if we decided only to use even numbers, we'd have a hard time with algebra. Well, the same thing happens with emotions and the algebra of relationships. In craving happiness, if we reject and devalue sadness, and a host of other valuable emotions as "*obstacles to happiness*," paradoxically we lose great data that would actually help us find a more profound and lasting happiness.

I recall a time, a long time ago actually, when I felt a large empty void. Even though I had many friends and opportunities to surround myself with people, the truth was I felt alone, even at those times. It was just me along with my persistent mind chatter asking me, "What is happiness? Have I ever really been happy?" My conditioned focus was always on anything outside of myself. It was always on my partner, my daughter, my work. This is where I looked to for my happiness. I was surrounded by all these wonderful people. I was successful and busy in my work and yet, I was not happy. I asked myself the next obvious question, "Why am I not happy?" The mind chatter was very revealing. It felt like a simultaneous rebellion and a gift of some sort, whereby I was being asked to change some aspects of my life, to see life through a different perspective.

Perhaps the loud and consistent mind chatter was because the action I was about to take was unusual for me. I was taking a two-year sabbatical and moving to Greece. Was this in search of happiness? I was not really certain. But I did know that doing something different would produce an entirely different perspective and outcome, and one I felt would serve me well.

On my journey through the process of self-discovery, I learned a lot about myself and happiness. First off, I learned that I was a "master pretender" at being happy. I also learned that walking around each day chanting, "I'm happy, I'm happy, I'm happy," was not going to get me a plaque in the "happiness hall of fame."

Over time, I experienced three types of happiness. First, I lived in my world of what I called surface happiness. It was a form of simple happiness—like a beautiful sunset, a delicious meal, or a coveted new dress. This state of happiness was in the moment, transient, and faded very quickly.

As I continued with my inner discovery work, I began to feel a more lasting happiness, one that was more balanced between present and future. I found that I could own this state of happiness and nothing outside of myself could take it away because this happiness no longer had attachments or needs and, therefore, was more sustainable.

Then there came a time that I experienced a much deeper happiness and one that has remained with me. It is more of a wholeness feeling—a connection to the very fabric of life. It's about feeling worthy of the incredible gifts and opportunities life provides. This profound sense of happiness also included a sense of balance that seemed to be intertwined with the benefits of truly knowing myself and its expression is linked to doing things that not only expressed myself but reflected who I am outwardly in positive ways.

The bigger issue is the mind is not free to be happy. The mind is acting from the *writing on our walls* and until we address and transform what is *written on our walls*, we will never experience the true essence of "profound happiness."

Here are some examples of powerful and quite common core patterns of behaviors that show up for many of us:

We say we are unhappy simply because we lose the ability to know and express what we really feel, and this becomes a major obstacle in our quest for happiness and our exchange of love. When cut off from our feelings, we are also cutting others off from important parts of our being. Some of us become unhappy when we do not receive the attention or love we think we need or we are afraid to accept love because we have identified being loved with some danger. In these cases, we might choose to not feel a love connection no matter how much others might love or respect us. When we do not know what we really feel, we often confront the others with the wrong emotions, which confuse and create unnecessary conflicts. Other times, we are afraid to express what we feel for fear of losing love or respect from others. Perhaps the *writing on our walls* has conditioned us to remain silent, which might have programmed us to feel that we lack self-worth or self-confidence.

There is a Buddhist concept that says, "Our unhappiness comes from our wants, attachments, needs, and expectations."

I agree, when we are attached to our wants and needs in order to feel safe, worthy and free, then we feel more frequently hurt and angry. When we have wants, needs, and expectations, we tend to push and pull the Life Force Energy in an attempt to force a particular outcome that we have become attached to. To accomplish the outcome in our favor, we might find our self totally ignoring the perspectives of others, or we might engage in some attempts to manipulate the outcome to fit our needs. Then if our needs do not get met, we tend to go into overwhelm and overreact to the circumstances that we ourselves created!

Other reasons for our unhappiness are that we seem to resist or even resent our experiences instead of accepting life as it comes. Or we are rushing through life without feeling things fully often ignoring our intuition to slow down and enjoy each moment. We may have become an expert at avoiding the present moment by looking to the past or trying to figure out our future. This causes us much unhappiness and we tend to become judgmental of things past or we suffer anxiety and worry about what will happen in our future. The truth is the past is gone and that our future is always created in each present moment!

In our pursuit of happiness, we sometimes find that we go looking for ourselves where we are not in order to feel happy. Often, we are prepared to make various alterations in our lives—sometimes even drastic ones with the hope that something else or someone else, or perhaps another job, or living in another country will make us happier. In such cases, we might seek to fill that emptiness by other means, such as overeating, drinking alcohol, drugs, over working, accumulating wealth or fortune, or being overly focused on sensual pleasures or activities. We might even lose ourselves in serving others with the hope that they will love us. We might seek to amass money and material objects believing this will bring us happiness. The problem is that we seldom obtain happiness in these ways. We will not solve the problem of unhappiness by seeking it in the outer world because happiness is an inside job!

The truth is that we tend to overly identify our self with who we think we are based on our programming and who we have been told we should be or what we have been told we should do. Whenever I hear the word "should," I know it is the writing on my wall! We tend to resist change and we are comfortable with our patterns because we are used to them. We feel safe within the boundaries of the writing on our walls. We fear change and we fear what is unknown to us.

The highest project we can devote our self to is self-reflection and self-discovery. The process of self-discovery requires work or even struggle to deal with these intricacies of human behavior. However, it can be a rewarding process when we can remain simply a curious observer. We are totally connected to all that exists, as we have always been. The only thing we've really lost is the Awareness of our connection. As we expand and become more aware, we find that we need less and less from the outer world and other people. We realize that security, love, and joy are innate qualities of being and they can't be lost—only forgotten.

The only difference between our happiness and our suffering is not the way things are in the moment, it's our response to this moment. It's our acceptance or rejection of this moment and what is arising in this moment. Imagine how different and happier our life would be if we did this one simple thing. Accept what is happening in each moment exactly as it is without wishing it would change in any way. Each moment cannot be other than what it is. Wishing it were different does absolutely nothing but make us suffer. To embrace reality is really quite wonderful, no matter what it is or how it appears to be.

By participating fully in life, welcoming our human idiosyncrasies, welcoming the fear as well as the safety, the sorrow as well as bliss, even the shame as well as pride, and by using all of our emotions as advisors and signals, we will find ourselves on an adventure to live life fully. In the end, unhappiness will seem like a phantom, something barely remembered. We will no longer limit ourselves to the pursuit of happiness. We will become the happiness we have been seeking.

*

Going Deeper

CR: Feelings are what we know experientially and not to be confused with our emotions. Emotions are what we feel with what we think we know. There is a difference. Your feelings are your perceptions of truth, but they may not be 'the truth.' In fact, they are an illusion. When we are unhappy, we often feel conflicted within. This conflict represents incongruences between what we think in the mind and what our heart knows.

The questions below are not always easy to answer, and many beginners to the process of self-discovery feel frustrated. Again, my suggestion is to try turning this frustration into genuine curiosity about getting to know yourself and others on a deeper level. Play with the mystery and wonder of all that is. Ask yourself the following:

What makes me happy?

What makes me unhappy?

What is it that is actually bothering me, triggering my unhappiness?

What do I feel? What are the emotions that I feel at this moment?

What do I believe consciously or subconsciously about myself or others which is causing me to feel unhappy?

What may have happened in the past which may have programmed me to believe these beliefs and are now causing my pain or unhappiness?

What is my lesson here? What do I need to change or learn?

How can I make this change in my mental emotional processes?

Journaling

CR: Begin a journal about your experience with happiness. Write about a moment in time when you felt happy. Write what you feel might have contributed to your happiness and describe the emotions you felt.

Next write about your experience with unhappiness. Try and determine what you might have felt that caused or contributed to that experience and try to identify all the emotions you felt. Be prepared not to have either all the questions or answers—remain open. Our tendency is to try to solve all the problems rather than allowing ourselves to have time to process and allow more questions to come up. End the journal entry with a question and the mind will continue to process the experience and the question.

Connect with Others

CR: Start a conversation with a friend or loved one sharing your experiences of both happiness and unhappiness and your insights from your journaling. Actively listen while encouraging the other person to tell their story of where they are on the happiness scale and why. Reflecting with your friend or partner, on both stories, discuss any missed opportunities to feeling profound happiness. Discuss how needs, attachments, or beliefs might have interfered with that happiness.

Milestones

CR: Are you in touch with what happiness means to you? Ask yourself daily if you are feeling happy? If not, why not? We want to get more specific when describing our happiness by using words that accurately describe our happiness. List all the experiences you've had that contributed to your current state of happiness. Take a moment to feel into your happiness and feel your gratitude. We celebrate these milestones by recognizing them and slowing down to take a moment to feel into them. Reality test them for what is true for you instead of simply answering with an automatic habitual response.

Making it Personal

DS: Life is beautiful, graceful, and marvelous. We are all gifted with precious gifts, a marvelous mind, an incredible body, and a warm loving and cosmic heart. Our body is our temple where our mind, soul, and spirit reside and through Awareness, we can concede our mind with our heart. Just like Nature that uses its forces to bring all the elements into equilibrium, we need to bring our precious gifts of life, body, mind, heart, and soul into perfect alignment. We must learn to live within the sacred rhythms of our loving heart that rise from the depths of our soul in silence and stillness.

We are born with a playful magical heart that keeps us joyful and enthusiastic. Just watch a little child going about his day, full of love and laughter, wonder and playfulness. As we get older, the world at large tries to change us into someone more acceptable. We need to keep looking at the world through the eyes of our childhood's heart and experience the purity and loveliness of our innocence.

The Greek philosopher, Aristotle, used the word Eudaimonia to describe happiness. Eudaimonia is the experience of our guardian spirit of joy in life. Over the course of life, I have experienced the virtue of Eudemonia in a number of different ways and many times I asked myself, "What prevents me from being happy?"

As a young boy in Greece, I had an Angel of Happiness that kept creating much joy within me and around me. When I became a teen-ager, I searched for happiness in the beauty of the outside world and soon afterwards found beauty and joy in the heart.

Later on, in life, I mistakenly connected happiness to outside sources, such as wealth and power, and for a number of years, I kept making automatic assumptions that the next moment would give me more happiness. Thus, following the dangling carrot theory and thinking that something better is right around the corner. At certain times, I was looking externally for reasons to be happy; seeking answers in the wrong places. Unfortunately, I had associated happiness with money and being acknowledged by others. But I came to the conclusion that this was an obstacle to my own happiness. I realized that I was not grateful enough and I was unappreciative of the present moment and kept robbing myself from the fullness, joy, and creative power of my heart. A time came when I asked if it was really worth struggling to satisfy the mind's need of how things should be and seeking approval of others. It was time for me to let go of the many desires and needs that kept depleting my energy and happiness.

I asked myself the following:

Didn't you have enough with the concept of adulthood and society's flow?

Once and for all, I felt I had had enough of trying to be more efficient and productive, searching for bigger, grandiose, and elaborate things. Blessed was that day when I realized that the most important thing in my life was to live fully and learn how to love well. Right at that moment, I knew that happiness did not rely on anything outside, but it was totally something within me.

Happiness is completely free from wealth, power, or any materialist goods. It solely depends on us. Oh, how happy I am now, knowing that there is a myriad of things that money can't buy and even if the whole Earth was mine, I would never be able to fully satisfy my mind's demands. Now I know that a meaningful life is not dependent on riches, fame, accomplishments, perfection, social affirmations, or even any external validation. Happiness is an attitude that simply depends on me.

Since this self-realization, I reconnected with the Angel of Happiness of my early youth and this led to a new discovery of the banquet of life full of plentiful pleasures. I accepted who I was and recognized my own accomplishments. I found joy in a number of things that were previously ignored or taken for granted. These included doing little things with great love, finding happiness in the value of friendship, love, playfulness, and the beauty of nature.

The Mind is the Map

Awareness is the Compass

The Critical Voice – The Writing on Our Wall

Our Life Force Energy

III

IV

V

II

The Mind is Not Free to be Happy

Understanding Our Patterns

I

VI

FINDING JOY

VII

Creating Our New Story

XII

The Present Moment

XI

VIII

X

IX

Living Life with Passion

Riding our Emotions to FREEDOM

Learning to Live Lightly

Creating a Solid Foundation

The Mind is the Map

Anxiety and fear are the stuff of the mind that focuses on what might or might not happen in the future even if that future is an hour from now. There is no other reality than the present moment. We cannot go to the store to buy something yesterday. Nor can we go now to buy something tomorrow. We can only act in the present. There is no other time but NOW.

FINDING
JOY

VII

The
Present
Moment

PART II:

CULTIVATING THE JOURNEY

"For those who have found the still point of entry, around which all—including themselves—revolves, everything is acceptable as it is, indeed, can be experienced as glorious and wonderful."

- Joseph Campbell

CHAPTER SEVEN

THE PRESENT MOMENT

CR: WHILE ON sabbatical, nesting in my apartment in Greece, my need for privacy was very strong. I was seeking seclusion in my own space, fostered by my desire to be alone to sort out my thoughts and learn to feel my feelings. I was hoping that this alone time would provide me with an opportunity to truly listen to what my soul wanted. Within my new space, perhaps I could summon the courage to explore the depths of what I thought I needed to be happy. I wondered if I deliberately filled my life with responsibilities that were not even mine and that my only participation in living my life was actually the distractions of other people.

I sat in every chair in my apartment, moving around from view to view, room to room, even bouncing on mattresses in my attempt to feel comfortable. Or was I trying to alleviate my fears and anxiety about me in my future? I was doing it again. I knew I was "resisting feeling things fully." What if I could simply sit with my feelings and acknowledge their existence? What if I could do that? What was the worst that could happen?

I wandered out to one of the three balconies wrapping the apartment. From two of them, I was able to see the sea. For me, a personal outdoor sanctuary that speaks to me has always been an important way for me to relax. I have learned to cultivate a sense of peace in my gardens over the years—a place where I surround myself in nature, beauty, and the Life Force Energy.

I no longer had a yard or a grassy corner, or a patio, but when it came to creating a garden, my creative potential was infinite. I decided to build myself a magnificent garden, right there on the balconies. I decided to blend wood and stone and fill my garden sanctuary with an abundance of flower pots overhanging the balcony railings. I placed full-size trees and statues in the corners and added a running water fountain at one end. I felt excited with my new project! I began taking measurements for the water fountain. I figured out how many trees, hanging baskets, and accessories were needed, and I planned where to place the outdoor furniture and, of course, a barbeque.

The potted trees and the water fountain were delivered and I set those in place. I hung the potted baskets and arranged the ornaments. Big box stores had just arrived in Greece and much to my dismay, everything needed to be assembled. Now I am about as handy as a tissue in the rain and realized that I actually had to build the garden furnishings. But I did and finally my garden sanctuary was complete. I was satisfied—at least for a little while.

Then it happened. I had run out of projects. I cried and I continued to cry for the next two days. I knew that it might take some time before I was able to let go of the past and create new memories. I had done it before and I could do it again. I looked around and I felt homeless, even after settling into my new place. I picked up one of my self-help books and put it down again after the first chapter. The last thing I wanted to read or think about, while sitting with these profound feelings of sadness, was anything resembling a bright side to my suffering. I experienced a new kind of "outdoorsy" in my new sanctuary, alone on the balcony getting tipsy on local wine, listening to old tunes that were chipping away at my already shattered self. I was not feeling great. In fact, I felt picked on by life—overwhelmed by the enormity of my life challenges and my suffering. Perhaps I was simply too exhausted to try and examine the situation. I felt heartbroken, disappointed, and angry.

My colleague from back home called and we had a chat. But really, I just whined and wined from the balcony. I was not used to having nothing to do. I'd been running on adrenaline with my businesses my entire life and the ride had completely stopped and I didn't feel the ground beneath me. And what was really scary was now that I was in Greece, I was not so sure I made the right decision. I didn't know if I could or even wanted to get off the ride of my busyness.

It was in that moment I realized my whole sense of myself had been based upon my doing. My colleague laughed and said, "Ah Christina, you're feeling!" And once again she encouraged me to "simply stay present with myself while learning to feel things fully and, yes it might feel awkward, but stay with the feelings." My feelings of awkwardness were already in place. The mind chatter had begun again, seemingly wanting to inform me as to, "What was I thinking? What was I doing?" I didn't have any answers. My intention was to set up a life I didn't feel the need to escape from!

What if my future was not something I simply stepped into or even got dragged into? I thought I was sure I made the right decision to change my life, but I found I was second guessing myself because my fear kept rearing and roaring at me. I was poisoning myself with my thoughts. I was arguing with myself over my self-imposed limitations. I should be excited that I got another opportunity to create my future, but I was not. Instead, I was fearful and the problem was, I didn't know what my future would look like.

The conflict within me vacillated up and down like tidal waves and continued for days. I was a leader, a planner, and an organizer. I worked hard all my life. I was a workaholic so I could afford to have what I considered a good life. Well actually, I spent all my time working, leaving no time to live the life I was working for. I decided to make things less complicated in my life. My "someday" was here. I had what I wanted and now I wanted something more. Instead of working on a "work in progress," as I did my business life, now I had become a work in progress, and a top priority one at that.

I was taught there were rules to follow to recreate a life, so I tried to understand what they were. In my present moment, I felt those rules didn't work for me and even more importantly, I wanted to know what's underneath all those layers of rules, society's rules, cultural rules, and even all my own rules. Where did the rules come from? Who makes them? Where did my own rules come from? Reality testing them, I realized they were not even mine. Some were my grandparents, my mother, my father, my teachers, and so on. Others—the rules that came from others—they were definitely not mine!

So what were my rules? What were my boundaries? Did I even have any I could claim as my own? Were any of them deal breakers or was I really a chameleon? I decided to find out what made me unhappy and then maybe I could discover what made me happy.

Above is an excerpt from my personal journals. During my own transformation, I came face-to-face with all my needs, wants, patterns and beliefs and I learned to see them all, to dissect them, to untangle their root causes, and to weed my garden of life. I learned that the only place I could retreat to was the moment at hand. I also learned that each present moment leads to the next moment and most important to the sanctity that is within each experience. Each moment contains an internal and external perspective, which opens us to the flow of life that carries us all. While at first my retreat seemed to be a refuge, soon facing and accepting my feelings and finding my way through moment by moment, it became a resource. It was during this time that I also experienced the difference between Joy and Happiness.

A good deal of our lives is spent in the pursuit of happiness, and happiness seems to come and go with a complimentary alignment of what we want to happen in our lives. This might be a release from difficulty or pain in our experiences or it might be an attachment to something external happening in our lives. Joy, on the other hand, seemed to be a very subtle slow awakening into the wonder of life and the joy of being alive. It was more a feeling of being connected to everything, experiencing life as a Holy vessel that holds us while we are in our pain and difficult moments.

A lot of our pain, bitterness, anger, shame and guilt has to do with our memories—even if those memories are about yesterday or this morning. If our memory was erased, we would not have any of those emotions. We experience them because we are allowing something that we are remembering, consciously or subconsciously, to stimulate our thoughts and feelings. Without a past, there can be no pain, anger, or guilt.

Anxiety and fear are the stuff of the mind about what might or might not happen in the future, even if the future is one hour from now. The present moment does not create such emotions and there is no other reality than the present moment. We cannot go to the store to buy something yesterday. Nor can we go now to buy something tomorrow. We cannot act in the past or in the future. We can only act in the present. Only in the present can we make decisions or respond to events or challenges. Only in the present can we exercise our free will to change our lives. The only point of power to create and change our lives is the present moment. There never was a time that was not NOW. There is no other time.

Life is always simply and exactly what it is in each moment. It cannot be other than this. Wishing it were different cannot make it different. There are certain things you can do to make some moment in the future different than it might be. But the future is not now. You will never find happiness in the future—for it is the all that is right now, with things exactly the way they are right now that creates our future. If you love the way things are in this moment, or at least completely accept them the way they are, you will be happy. If you don't, you will suffer, wishing things were different.

Our senses are another point of reference in the present. The heart is beating, the lungs are breathing, as life keeps engaging us—the light of our soul is visible, real, and authentic—fully engaging in each moment without pretense or illusion. When our senses are stimulated, we can temporarily let go of focusing consciously on the past and future. Of course, the subconscious egoic mind will still be preoccupied with the past and future until it is healed of this habitual tendency.

For you see, when our mind is preoccupied with the past or future, we tend to lose the joy and creativity of the present. We have less energy and clarity with which to make decisions and to perform our tasks. If we feel that we have less power in the present, it is because we are lost in the mind stuff, lost in the past and future.

To be a soul, living in this world, we must practice and participate in the wisdom of our hearts while coming alive in a limitless journey of our human experiences. Living in the present is enhanced by focusing on the present, our Life Force Energy, our senses, and our consciousness. We can learn to cultivate our ability to be witnesses of our energy, senses, thoughts, emotions, and experiences. This state of Awareness allows our consciousness to experience a degree of detachment from our thoughts and feelings so that we can experience the peace and bliss that are behind and beyond the mind. There is a place within each of us that has not been touched by pain. Awareness gives us access to this place.

Imagine how your life would be if you accepted every moment of your life as the absolute perfection that it is. Imagine if you stopped wishing any moment were different than what it is right now. If you stopped wishing you were in a relationship or a different relationship, wished you had more money, success or fame, wished your health were better, wished you were enlightened, wished anything were different from the way it is right now. What would happen if instead you simply accepted the great gift of this moment exactly as it is? Just imagine this for a moment. I don't think it will take long for you to see that the result of doing this will bring great joy, happiness, satisfaction, and fulfillment because it will be in alignment with truth, with reality.

Shifting from happiness to joy is a state beyond even profound happiness. It is beyond happiness in the sense that it lives inside of us and has nothing to do with anything "out there." Joy is a sensation that overcomes us as we experience Oneness. Sometimes in our search for happiness, we block the real joy of our placement in the Universe. It's that place in our center where we live lightly and securely, in the present moment, embracing and welcoming the nature of all things as they are. Such humility awakens a heightened sensitivity of our heart space and returns us to the experience of Joy, of living Heaven on Earth.

We often hear stories of being present and entering the moment of Joy and this has been explored from many vantage points. I feel it has something to do with the action of slowing down long enough to align the pace of our thinking mind with the pace of our feeling heart. When aligned, these in turn align our ability to see and hear with clarity giving way to a fresh perception.

Feeling into our experiences is the process of insight giving way to presence, matching us to the rhythm and the pace of creation itself. Insight is the awakening of spirit and presence—not the other way around. In fact, perhaps too much time is wasted in pursuing happiness over simply experiencing JOY.

Joy is always found in the present moment, and in order to experience it, we will need to learn to live in the present without the pain, bitterness, anger or guilt of the past or the anxiety or fear concerning the future. If we examine our unpleasant emotions, we will discover that they are always based on the past or future.

Although our minds can wander at times, creativity is another way to experience the present. When creating, usually such activities engage our mind in the present as we enjoy the creative process. Creativity also leads to states of inspiration that bring excitement and happiness.

Another anchor to the present is the Awareness of our energy body. We can also focus on the Life Force Energy in and around our bodies while in a state of relaxation, so that even while moving, we are aware of that energy. Being aware of this energy in and around our body allows us to be fully present, and it is also a window to purer higher levels of consciousness that lay behind and beyond our mind.

As we begin to access our pure consciousness, which is Awareness without an object of Awareness, we begin to feel peace in the present. Our higher level of consciousness is pure, immutable, and blissful. In the present moment of Awareness, of inner bliss, lies our true lasting JOY.

Pure consciousness is our essence and is always in a state of peace and bliss, but it is usually masked by disturbances of the mind. However, the peace of JOY exists even when there is disturbance in the mind. It is always there, just as the white light behind the film of the projector remains white and formless no matter what is appearing on the screen. The mind will need to be silenced in order to experience that peace. In order to experience a steady form of JOY, we will need to let go of the past and future and develop Awareness of the present and of ourselves as consciousness rather than as bodies and minds.

We will also want to experience the present moment as it is and not as it is distorted by our beliefs, fears, emotions, and prejudices.

In general, we do not see what is, but rather what we believe is. Our beliefs distort our perception of reality and interpret it in subjective ways dependent on our subconscious conclusions based on our previous experiences. Our beliefs may well be the obstacles that limit the beauty of the present moment with these subjective interpretations.

If we want to experience the joyful divinity of every present moment, we will need to let go of another basic obstacle—the illusory feeling of separateness created by our senses; when in fact we are spirit, energy and matter connected with the all that is. This feeling of being separate from others, and the forces around us, cause us to fear and develop defense mechanisms that seriously obstruct our happiness.

If we find ourselves living this lower energy self and feeling lost in the midst of pain and hurt, ask for guidance. Simply pray and give it to God. It is only in that moment that we can truly have an expectation. This is what I call expectant waiting, whereby we exchange our feebleness for faith that turns to prayer and we engage God with the full bluntness of our emotions and pain. It is in this moment that we have the only absolute expectation knowing that all is well. We actively expect to be restored and we don't need to know how, what or when. This is where we will find true and lasting Joy.

DS: It is so true that our mind is guided by the past and keeps contemplating the future. Essentially our mind is on constant interpretation of the past and in survival mode towards the future. However, when we rise above our thoughts and emotions, we begin to realize that between the perception of the past and wonderful dreams of the future, lay the magnificence of the present. This is the most important moment of our life, one that resonates with our soul-spirit experienced in our body.

Ask yourself the following:

How important is freedom from the constantly thinking mind?

Would you like your life to move like the flow of water currents on a smooth river along the rhythms of nature and beauty?

Do you want to live life with passion?

If your answer is yes to the above, then let life unfold within the present moment.

Falling in love with life means falling in love with the present moment. It is experiencing the Life Force Energy of your breath—listening to your heart beating and filling your mind and heart with lovely rhythms, pitches, and harmonies.

Our five senses are here to inspire and vitalize our ability to stay in the present moment and to receive pleasure from everywhere and everyone. Our sight embraces the variation of light. Our sound that of creativity. Our touch explores every feeling and our smell picks up the sweetest nectar from every flower. Being in the present feels like an eternally flowing river of trust and Just like the water is the carrier of each and every rhythm of life, we allow our body and mind to experience the eternal flow of the present moment.

Our soul resonates with all forms of life and picks up marvelous vibrations, which reflect our beauty and loveliness at each moment. Just like all of us, I kept wondering how, with all the busyness of life and a fast-moving world filled with multiple events and demands, I would be able to remain in the present moment? Learning how to be present to each moment helped me to develop a sense of trust and also to be present to myself. This meant letting go of any future desires that kept robbing me of this moment. Feeling presence in the present moment was as simple as feeling the ground beneath me, listening to the sounds of the wind, and the birds and moving with the ebb and flow of the tropical songs of waves.

Numerous times during the day I close my eyes and experience myself to be like a leaf afloat a crystal-clear lake of stillness. Feeling the soothing water flow and easiness in my back, my neck, and my head, relaxes me from the turbulence of life. Just like the water of life that renounces every self-quality to become a generation of pure forms, I renounce any disturbing thoughts and surrender to the tranquility of the present moment.

When I contemplate on nature, nature contemplates on me and sees me through my very own eyes. Nature purifies my soul and heals me from society's adverse flow, dependencies, and needs. Nature guides me to live mindfully in the present moment. To be in tune with the natural flow is to align with its rhythm and experience the powerful energy of natural elements.

My soul yearns for freshness and beckons my earthly beauty. Nature has always been a big part of my life. I was magically connected to its beauty, blessed with it as a child experiencing the presence of the natural world. Nature's richness encircles all of the seasons. We are all born and die to the light of the summer and the darkness of the winter. When I am with the natural world, I feel connected to the beauty and blissful harmony of the trees, plants, grass, flowers, and animals and all that is contained by the elements of fire (sun), water, air and earth. During my journey in nature, all my attention is given to that moment and I am totally present, happy, and joyous.

The power of the natural world is my key to the portal of the present moment. Nature is my garden of love. Just like the powerful aroma of a flower offers its fragrance, nature fills my heart with gratefulness and appreciation. When I am in the natural world, I am open to what is happening and at the same time contained. There is no need for preconceived notions or multiple thoughts, just being in the present experience. Nature is my guide to entering the present moment. When a thought attempts to pull me to the past or future, I rest in the natural stillness, beauty, peace, and positive energy.

The idea of being in the present moment guided me towards the creation of a garden of love. I planted my own flowers as a means of appreciation, love, joy, and wholeness. Their vibrant and harmonious colors gave off unique and elegant fragrances that became symbols of the beauty of the present moment. Caring for a garden that I had neglected for years became the space of soothing painful feelings and a form of mindfulness to the present moment. Being aware of how my rose tree was drawing light from the radiant sun, water from the sublime rain, and moonlight transforming into something beautiful inspired me to use my Life Force Energy to fill my body and heart with inner joy and happiness. And just like the rose that adorns itself in order to adorn the garden, I learned to use my internal radiance to shine beauty to all.

Nature is always present, and if we open our heart to reach out and receive her, we will give ourselves the gift of mindful living and the present of NOW. There is always an inter-play between our Awareness and the Universal Energetic Life Force. Tuning into it requires that we create the capacity to remain in the present moment.

*

Going Deeper

CR: Each of our lives speaks a language of its own, one that no one else really knows. We have been touched by many experiences even where we did not realize we were touched. Some experiences left wounds and distorted templates on the subconscious and unconscious mind that we don't even know about because we have been conditioned to resist feeling things fully. We must accept the truth of what is and translate the mystery that has been *written on our wall* and transform all that we think though the knowing heart. Our experiences in life ask each of us to enter the humble process of self-discovery, again and again, so the act of living life reveals and untangles both the questions and the answers. Each life is a unique puzzle, a mystery to be solved, and each of us is an alchemist.

When we are thrust into our experiences in life, we often feel conflict within. It represents incongruences between what we think in the mind and what the heart knows. The mind has a thought and this thought creates an emotion. The moment we stray from the present moment, either to the past or to the future, we create a tension between two places, where we are and where we are thinking from. This splits our attention from the present moment, and this is where the choice points and clarity reside.

To uncover the conflict and the struggle you find yourself in, here are some questions you might ask yourself:

Where is my thinking from—past or future?

What emotion am I feeling with my thinking?

What do I believe or what fundamental understanding do I have about my thinking?

Did I choose this thinking or was this something I was taught?

Do I value this thinking? If so, why? If not, can I let it go?

How can I remain integral in my Awareness?

What are some of the obstacles preventing me from staying in my present moment?

How can I stay aligned in the present moment?

How can I make a practice of living and knowing Oneness?

Journaling

CR: In very real ways we are drawn to experiences that teach us what we need to know and the gift of the experience might be waiting on the threshold of your curiosity. Consider journaling an experience that touched you with such a great depth of emotion that you were not able to stay in the present moment. What was preventing you?

Now journal an experience whereby you were able to remain calm in your present moment. What was the experience asking of you beyond the pain and suffering?

What was contained within the experience of the present moment that helped you grow?

How can you develop and maintain integrity; advance consistency with what you think, feel, say, and do—in your present moment?

Take some time to ponder and process your experience of the present moment. Assess and reassess.

If any actions are necessary, ask yourself what steps can I take to be proactive?

Connect with Others

CR: Start a conversation with a friend or loved one sharing your experience and your insights from your journaling. Now tell a story of a time where you paid too much attention to the mind stuff and were unable to remain in full Awareness to what was unfolding in your life in a present moment. In retrospect, describe the missed opportunity to see a deeper meaning of the experience and to initiate change and by not living in the present moment, how might the experience have misled you or impacted you in a negative way. Now perform active listening and ask your friend or loved one if they would like to share their experience of a similar nature.

Milestones

CR: We will all encounter endless life experiences. Our constant cease-less efforts to engage in living our life fully involves a commitment to keep what is true, while living in the present moment. This is how we are able to align our self with the higher frequencies of the Life Force Energy in all things. This is a never-ending practice of tuning our inner self to the mysteries that surround us. In doing so, it is important to celebrate the milestones of honoring what we are experiencing, and by keeping only what is real and visible in the present moment.

The Mind is the Map

Our emotions are powerful and can either guide us towards our higher consciousness or keep us captive in lower levels of energy, such as fear, anxiety, and doubt. Riding our emotions to freedom requires that we understand the interplay between the mind to the heart and from fear to faith, as we learn to live more fully from our heart.

FINDING JOY

VIII

Riding our Emotions to FREEDOM

PART II:

CULTIVATING THE JOURNEY

"Emotion is the chief source of all becoming-conscious.
There can be no transforming of darkness into light
and of apathy into movement without emotion."

- Carl Jung

CHAPTER EIGHT

RIDING OUR EMOTIONS TO FREEDOM

CR: AT OUR present stage of evolution, emotions are a main source of our Life Force Energy and creative power. Properly used, they can guide us to the truth and to ever greater states of freedom and happiness. This, however, is seldom the case for most of us. We tend to allow our emotions, especially the fear-based ones, to seriously limit our freedom and happiness. This might be because we don't know how to use them. When making reference to the mind, I am not only speaking to our thoughts, I am including the emotions as well. We are energy beings and many negative lower energy emotions show up as illness in the physical body as a reflection of the mind stuff.

Emotions help us know what is important in "mature judgment" as well as ethical decision-making. They tell us where we stand, who we can trust, who to push away, and who to embrace. They also remind us to take care of ourselves and each other, and fuel both resistance and innovation.

Perhaps we are by human design programmed to feel emotions as painful and unity as pleasant. This wisely creates the foundation for our evolution and movement towards a more loving reality. Our unhappiness is caused by our lack of contact with our inner higher nature and true self. We long for our true nature, which is ultimately divine. Our true self is the one universal consciousness, which is also the true self of all other beings and of all creation. We will never solve the problem of our unhappiness until we reunite with our true divine self.

I spoke earlier about how change entered my life suddenly and painfully causing huge shifts in my internal and external world. I have read somewhere that learning our lessons in life goes something like this. First, we get the postcard regarding our life lesson. Then we get the letter. Then we get the package. Then we get the box. And finally, we get the crate. Eventually through the repetition of our life experiences, we will get the message!

Once again looking back into my journals, "The mind chatter was very revealing, fascinating, and loud. It was full of my perceptions of what I should do—what can I do verses what can't I do, and what am I afraid to do based on my "what if's and "yes buts." All this noise was because the action I was about to take. To go to Greece was unusual for me. The act of leaping into my future without a handle on my present and a mind full of my past. I seemed to have no direction. I just had a mind full of thoughts and issues, but no concrete solutions. I mentioned earlier that my mind chatter revealed that I was a jumble of perceived needs, urges, and emotions and I knew I was resisting feeling things fully.

Well, perhaps the real truth was that I was resisting placing any attention on me in my life at all. It felt more like I was running away from something, instead of towards something. For the first time in my life, I had no plan. I felt I wanted to be carried for a while as I was filled with an intense uncertainty about what was next for me.

More importantly, I did not know what I wanted. This was that first moment in my timeline of transformation where I decided to let go of everything and just be me and living my life as Spirit, it began to unravel before me. I began practicing mindfulness coupled with what I had learned about Emotional Intelligence. I put faith in myself and God and I just knew I would be fine. After some time, I began to feel everything and to perceive things through a cleaner lens. I began to trust what was real for me and I found the courage to express what my truth was.

It is from my direct experiences that I can say that mindfulness is something that can be learned along with Emotional Intelligence. It felt to me like the mind might be condemned by its very own programming to lose its peace, happiness, and love when confronted by situations, behaviors or events which it interprets as threatening to the fulfillment of its basic needs. Its logic, in such moments, is powerless against the force of these deeply ingrained reflex emotional mechanisms. Being attached to certain external conditions for one's happiness is the surest way to lose happiness when those factors are threatened in any way, be it in the past, present or future. Until we are free from the control of our obsolete mental programming and thought forms, we will be susceptible to our inner negativity and our automatic, habitual programming, which at times creates an unpleasant atmosphere for ourselves and those around us.

Observing our emotions is as important as observing our thoughts. We can free ourselves from the pain of negative emotions by no longer identifying who we are or think we are from the mind or the Ego. When we no longer give a free rein of power to the mind, our true nature reveals itself. We are unable to live our higher vibrational emotions, such as love, joy, and peace until we free ourselves from the dominance of our mind.

Some negative emotions are a disturbance and there are also

particular positive ones that seem to reside beyond the negative emotions on a much deeper level at the core of our true essence. As we explore our entire range of emotions, we will be able to feel the undisturbing positive emotions, the ones that do not cause us pain and suffering, and they, of course, vibrate at much higher energetic frequencies.

Most of us have not realized the truth of who we are and why we are here and yet the realization of our true self is the solution. We are not simply physical bodies; we are actually spiritual beings expressing ourselves through these bodies and minds. Through our experiences here on this earth, we have a challenge to see if we can remember our true spiritual nature. From birth, we are programmed to identify with our individual body to the exclusion of all others. We learn to fear physical and emotional pain and we view ourselves as separate from others.

Many of us live as if we are completely unaware of our immortality. We are powerful beings and yet we feel weak. The truth is that we create our own realities and yet we feel that we are victims of circumstances external to our being. We are pure love, but we get overwhelmed by emotions like fear, hurt, bitterness, and anger. We live with low self-esteem, doubt, self-judgment, and self-rejection because we have not yet realized that we are one with the divine incarnated in a temporary form. We live the illusion instead of the reality and all of these illusions create a reality totally inferior to the one we deserve—the one of our true self. For you see, we all deserve much more love, peace, happiness, abundance, harmony, and pleasure in our lives.

DS: Indeed, dear friend, our emotions are powerful and can either guide us towards our higher consciousness or keep us captive in lower levels of energy, such as fear, anxiety and doubt. Our mind's programming has an inheritance of fear. I recall moments in my own life when I had felt trapped—times when I believed that I was concealed inside a big block fear and loss. Our frightening images can be transformed into beautiful complete creations with the use of our brave heart. The choice is ours and it is either the door to the room that leads to light and freedom, or the door to the room that leads to darkness and entrapment.

Practicing Emotional Intelligence and Awareness makes us conscious of our thoughts and feelings and raises our pneuma-Life Force Energy to a Universal conscious intelligence beyond any limits. Riding our emotions to freedom requires that we understand the interplay between mind to heart and fear to faith. Fear has an inherent intelligence of protection and we can use it as a way of self-discovery, which gives us an opportunity to reality test our experience and to determine what is real for us. Otherwise, fear will isolate us from the most purely formed living thing on earth, our heart. Often enough I ask myself, "Do I live life by being fearful of this world or do I live with ultimate faith and love?" When the force of faith flows within me, I am instantaneously connected to the courage of my heart. I experience the force of faith like a light dwelling from the seat of my heart, an internal light that doesn't go out, but pervades, infuses, and animates all life.

We are given many opportunities in life to undergo a shift in the mind's programming, to realize the power of our higher nature, and to become co-creators with the Universe. Our higher nature and higher intelligence is like a golden mist swirling out to our multi-colored being and connecting us to our divinity. All we have to do is realize that the entire Universe is within us and allow our thoughts to be shifted from the limitations of the mind to the cosmic capacity of the heart. That is when we will experience the most joyful life.

CR: Yes, Dimitrios, when we observe the mind, we will find that our thinking creates our emotions and our reactional behavior patterns and that they are designed to keep the pain of these lower-level emotions running in our lives, giving us the opportunity to live and grow into higher levels of consciousness not only for ourselves, but for those around us. When we become truly conscious of these pains and patterns, we can initiate change and the pain will begin to dissolve. The instant that we observe the pain and emotion, try to feel the energy of that emotion within your body. It is best to not add any more thoughts to this field of energy. Thoughts are of the mind and we are now focused within the body. Place your attention on the field of energy within your body. Simply remain in Awareness and stay present with it and you will find it will begin to dissipate. Notice how the identification with this pain is dissipating and feel a higher level of conscious Awareness move into its place.

This is what is known as Mindful Presence. You are now operating from a place of Awareness as the witness or the observer in the present moment. This means the mind can no longer use you. It can no longer replenish the old thoughts or add new thoughts because you have made a conscious choice in the present moment to remove your energy and place it elsewhere. You have activated your will to find your inner most strength and you have used this power. All it took was for you to become the observer in present time and to feel the energy of the emotions until there was nothing left to feel and now it can no longer control your thinking mind.

This process is the action of one who is emotionally intelligent and it takes practice. But it can be so simple that it can be taught to a child. Once we understand the basic principle of being present as the observer of what is going on within us and also understand that by simply being willing to experience it fully, we will have grasped the most important tool in the tool box of self-realization and transformation. Only you can do this. No one can do this for you. But sometimes we can find someone who is willing to hold a loving space for us that can be helpful and will accelerate the process.

There is no need to focus on becoming free of the mind stuff. We need only remain present by being the observer of the mind in the present moment. As long as the unobserved mind is controlling our lives, we are creating unnecessary pain for our self. STOP doing that. The more we honor and accept the present moment, the pain and suffering from the egoic mind will cease. It helps to also remember that the present moment is all there really is. The past is gone and the future is unknown. So how can we possibly make rational or logical choices and decisions based on that timeline? We can't. The only choice points we will ever have are the present moment. It is best to make the now moment the primary focus of our lives. Surrender all else and show up in the present moment. Say YES to life and begin to see how life will respond in a new and supportive way. Always accept what is and make any choices in the present moment and from a place of love.

It is clear that on our evolutionary path we have taken on the challenge of conscious evolution. It is clear that we have been given the gift of the mind as the map to understanding the process to achieve this goal. The mind offers us the ability to pay witness to ourselves and to a greater extent for the divine purpose of eliminating all sense of separation from each other and from God. The fact that we even have emotions challenges us to choose freely to overcome fear and to forgive and love others and ourselves. We have choices and the free will to make those choices. We can choose peace over fear, forgiveness over bitterness and resentment, compassion over judgment, and to see the truth of who we are over the illusion of who we think we are. We can choose to be authentic over what others think we should be or would like us to be. The ultimate choice is Love over Fear. All of the rest is the stuff of the mind.

The path of living a fruitful and happy life is a rite of passage to the higher realms of consciousness. It is not an easy road filled with the sweetness of life, nor is it a fearful path. It is completely benevolent and authentic in its essence. It is a liberating quest for truth. Often, we can touch it for brief moments through meditation, reflection, mindfulness, mantras, and so forth, but it is hard to live in this space for long. The mind gets triggered, and when it does, it brings forth all the old programming and emotions. This includes any childhood survival skills, along with any childlike conclusions we came to about the original experience and far too often, we find ourselves deep within our inner and outer experiences of conflict.

The mind is the map and by using the compass of Awareness, we can work with the mind to bring these old experiences to light and love within the heart for transformation. This is the path to living a spiritual existence with constancy. By observing the mind through acts of Awareness, this will ultimately lead us to create new automatic habitual programming and behaviors that allow us to live from the heart and the truth of who we are. That truth is we are One with God, one with each other, and one with all that is.

This is our test and the time is now. We can remember our true nature and the course of the true nature of our parents, spouse, children, siblings, coworkers, friends, and enemies. We can remember the true nature of divine beings that have incarnated into other religions, nationalities, races, genders or political or philosophical ideologies. We have come with the challenge of breaking through the veil of our self-imposed ignorance and the emotions and life situations that humanity has created by those illusions.

DS: Observing and identifying the originality of our emotions is one of the most important gifts we can give to ourselves. Understanding emotions is like a form of art. In the same way that Phidias and Michelangelo looked into a block of stone and discovered its beauty and essence, we have the capacity to look inside our mind and detect our unresolved emotions.

Our habitual patterns are deeply buried within us and just like unfinished pieces of marble require smoothening off their sharp rough edges, so do we. We soften, polish, and transform our beliefs and emotions and bring them to the surface towards the creation of a magnificent spectrum of life and shine our true light everywhere.

Old wounds are caused by painful experiences that remain in our memories and return to play out when we get triggered. Wounds are formed in the context of relationships from an early age and we tend to follow our learned habitual responses similar to our initial reactions to the old experiences. We keep carrying them in our mind as counter weights and they not only keep holding us down, but they influence our decisions and behaviors in our present moments and often in conflicting ways.

I had a need to be respected, and every time I did not receive that respect, I felt mistreated. Perhaps, I had an old belief of some kind that caused me to care too much about what others were thinking or saying about me or perhaps, I had a need for some outside validation.

My need for respect kept showing up in different areas of my life. This appeared in my personal relationships and in my work environment.

My heart's desire became to ride this unpleasant emotion to freedom and clear this pattern of not being respected in any future situations that would limit my potential.

I remember being a happy child. My mom was one of those people who understood and exercised the principles of unconditional love. Her loving heart never saw right or wrong, and she never had a need for external respect or being acknowledged by others. She was simple, soft, humble, and flexible. In regards to my relationship with my father, I can't say much because I hardly knew him. He moved to the States after I was born and passed away when I was ten years old. Mom always said that he was a happy, simple, and loving person too and without any strict rules. In addition, Mom and I lived next to a number of close relatives who always surrounded us with love and laughter.

So, my need for respect had to come outside our home and from a different environment. Perhaps it was from someone else in an attempt to change me into something acceptable to society norms.

I asked myself the following:

Where did my need for respect come from?

What is it that I believe about respect?

What may have happened in the past which may have programmed me to believe that I needed respect from others?

What was bothering me and kept triggering this feeling of not being respected?

How important was my need to be acknowledged and be accepted by others?

Was the need for respect coming from an old wound? If so, how was I wounded and by whom?

Our school environments can be responsible for many of our earlier and deepest wounds. Like all of us, our teachers have wounds and beliefs that are projected onto students. I remembered some of my teachers in high school whose words and actions were not appropriate for the class. Specifically, I recall a teacher who kept yelling at the students. He was a teacher of religion, but instead of teaching God's love, he was verbally and physically abusive and in addition to his angry behavior, he always demanded respect.

I questioned myself and thought, "If being fearful of the teacher had resulted in a wound?

How deep was this wound?

What were my thoughts and perceived barriers supporting my belief that I needed respect?"

I observed the old experience and afterwards I examined that experience and the teacher's request of demanding respect. I witnessed the entire process through a series of images and thoughts. I noticed what I was saying in my own mind.

I asked myself, "How was my old pattern of feeling disrespected affecting my life in my present moment?

What was the mental process I was following? What were my underlying beliefs about disrespect that kept disempowering me?

Why was I asking for respect and acceptance from others?

How could I release my need to be respected?

How could I transform my old childhood wound by living it through the warm capacity of my heart?

Was my need for respect by others something within my power?"

I discovered that it was not. The truth is, if someone has an existing pattern of disrespect, most likely they disrespect many others around them.

I don't believe there is something wrong with desiring respect and worthiness, but when we attach it to each situation and demand it from everyone without taking into account their *writing on the wall,* we become like the cat chasing its tail to find happiness.

Sometimes, we are deeply wounded by the very same people we love as well as those who love us. Wounds that have not healed will remain within us, sitting right behind our thoughts and feelings until they are transformed. Healing comes when we stop defending our beliefs, hiding them, or projecting them onto others.

Freeing ourselves from an old wound feels like a golden mist. We can undo the Ego's hold and lower nature of our emotions by using the power of our witness. We can cure and heal our wounded earthly self by connecting to the divine wisdom of our inner physician and healer.

Spiritual healing opens us up to higher degrees of light and promotes conscious thinking and the healing power of ourselves through the agape of our heart. We must be willing to feel things fully and ride all of our emotions to freedom, leading us to the alignment of our local self to our higher nature, higher intelligence, and higher consciousness.

Going Deeper

CR: Emotions are one of the main things that derail communications and persuasions. Once people start getting upset at one another, rationalism goes out of the window. If you can identify and control your own emotions, you have good chance of avoiding conflict. If you can sense the emotions of others, you have a better opportunity to resolve the issue. And, of course, it all starts with you and your own emotions. The ability to balance emotion and reason in making decisions leads to good decisions. Emotion should not be abandoned, lest cold and callous decisions are made. Nor should logic be abandoned unless you want a wishy-washy outcome.

Emotional literacy means being able to label emotions precisely. This includes the emotions of others and especially your own emotions. It also means being able to talk about emotions without getting overly emotional or (as happens with many people) denying them. Emotional literacy is not using 'I feel…' statements to offer opinions, ideas, etc. Thus, 'I feel that is a good idea' is not emotional literacy, whist 'I feel angry' is. Being emotionally self-aware means knowing how you feel in "real time."

Self-knowledge is the first step in being able to handle emotions. If you can see them and name them, then you at least have a chance to do something about them. Empathy is the ability to feel and understand the emotions of others. If you can empathize, you can engender trust, as people desperately want to be understood at the emotional level. Emotional Intelligence means taking primary responsibility for your own emotions and happiness. You cannot say that others "made" you feel the way you feel. Although they may be instrumental, the responsibility is yours. There is no such thing as someone else made you do it. Emotional Intelligence is a neat metaphor that borrows from the notion of IQ. It implies that some people are better at handling emotions than others. It also hints that you might be able to increase your Emotional Intelligence. Practically it offers a useful set of guidelines for doing just this. It also means appreciating and accepting differences between people, accepting that we have different priorities and capabilities around emotion.

Everyone experiences primary and secondary emotions. If you're finding it hard to differentiate your feelings or you're feeling emotionally detached, then getting help doing so is essential to living a full connected life. Living a life that isn't full of emotion, or consists of compromised emotional responses that are disrupting, is unnecessary and often lonely. Primary emotions are more transient than secondary emotions, which is why they're less complicated and easier to understand. The first thing we feel is directly connected to the event or stimulus but as time passes, we struggle to connect the same emotion with the event because our emotions have changed. Secondary emotions are much more complex because they often refer to the feelings you have about the primary emotion. These are learned emotions, which we start understanding by coping parents or others as we grow up. For example, when you feel angry you may feel ashamed afterward, or when you feel joy, you may feel relief or pride. Examples of secondary emotions include: "fear leads to anger, anger leads to hate, hate leads to suffering."

A secondary emotion is one that isn't a reaction, but a response to understanding the initial reaction. Secondary emotions can also be divided into instrumental emotions. These are unconscious and habitual. We learn instrumental emotions as children as a form of conditioning. When we cry, a parent comes to soothe us. So, we learn to use the facial expressions and responses associated with crying when we need that soothing or sense of security. Many toddlers are very adept at using instrumental emotions to get their way with anger. A toddler throws a tantrum, and parents give in to make them quiet, but as we grow, we learn that this behavior isn't appropriate or we become spoiled and manipulative. By not learning the correct secondary emotional response, it leaves the person distant and emotionally detached from those around them.

From a place of playfulness and genuine curiosity ask yourself the following:

What is it that is actually bothering me, triggering these emotions?

What do I feel? What are the emotions that I feel at this moment?

What do I believe (consciously or subconsciously) that are forcing me to feel these emotions?

What may have happened in the past that may have programmed me to believe these beliefs and what is now causing my pain or unhappiness?

What is my lesson here? What do I need to change or learn?

How can I make this change in my mental emotional processes?

Journaling

CR: Begin a journal about your experience with an emotion you are dealing with that causes you pain or frustration. Reflect back on your life to your earliest memory you have of feeling this emotion. See if you can discover the belief you had or the root cause underlying the emotion. Reality check to see if this is truly what you believe or is it someone else's belief *written on your wall*. Be prepared not to have either all the questions or answers—remain open. Our tendency is to try to solve all the problems rather than allowing ourselves to have time to process and allow more questions to come up. And again, as in previous chapters, although it may seem painful and not efficient even when we feel sure that we have the answer in our mind, it is often best to complete the journal entry with a question rather than an answer. This question will then work in the subconscious mind calling forth answers, intuition (tuition from within), inspiration, and guidance from within.

Connect with Others

CR: Start a conversation with a friend or loved one sharing your experience and your insights from your journaling. Do active listening while encouraging the other person to tell their story of where they are with their emotions. Reflect with your friend or partner on both stories and discuss any missed opportunities to identifying and feeling their emotions fully and how needs, attachments, or beliefs might have interfered with the outcome of their experience.

Milestones

CR: Few of us have a very intimate contact with feeling our emotions. When someone asks, "What we are feeling," we often answer vaguely, "bad, unhappy, upset, disturbed, and negative." We want to get more specific when describing our emotional state by using words which accurately describe the emotion we feel. Each time you take a moment to feel into your emotions and name them accurately, you have reached another milestone. Celebrate these milestones by recognizing them and slow down to take a moment to feel into what is true for us instead of simply answering with an automatic habitual response.

The Mind is the Map

When the foundation of our life is healthy, it expands and supports our life fully. We all want to feel secure in our lives, but what many of us perceive as security does not exist. True security is not found in the outer material world, nor is it found in our relationships with others. It is our inner security that regulates us and gives us a sense of well-being.

FINDING JOY

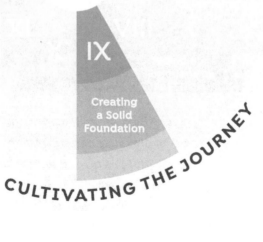

IX

Creating
a Solid
Foundation

PART II:

CULTIVATING THE JOURNEY

"*The most excellent and divine counsel, the best
and most profitable advertisement of all others,
but the least practiced, is to study and learn
how to know ourselves. This is the foundation of
wisdom and the highway to whatever is good.*"

- Pierre Charron

CHAPTER NINE

CREATING A SOLID FOUNDATION

C R: BUILDING A good strong foundation anchors our Life Force Energy in the physical plane. It ensures our survival and the quality of the life we live. We thrive well with constancy and we function well with stability in our lives. When the foundation of our life is healthy, it expands and supports our life fully. We can take on more responsibilities, be more creative, and even more playful. A healthy foundation is flexible, and at the same time, enjoys the daily rhythms of life. This stability allows us to be more patient as our life unfolds—less reactive and less volatile to what is external to our being as we learn to accept life as it is.

A strong foundation also helps us to maintain our spiritual connection when the winds of change blow in our lives. We want to create a foundation that is as strong as the concrete foundations of a house and can hold our life in place. Without a strong foundation, the irregularities and mishaps of life will toss us about and wreak havoc in our lives. Our Spirit will not survive well with constant chaos and we will be like a feather in the wind.

One of the most important lessons in life is to learn that we always take our self with us, leaving no parts of our multi-dimensional self behind. Our energetic footprint of who we are remains with us eternally. Our experiences in life remain with us always and there is both positive and negative energy within us that we can discover only by revisiting these experiences from a place of Awareness. The feeling is no longer the same when it comes the second time. If it was a negative experience, we have the opportunity to transform the energy field and, in most cases, it dissipates through the Awareness of its return and we begin to see that the sum total of who we think we are is not what we experienced. It is what we imagined we were living. It is our destiny to fully immerse ourself in the great experience called life and to live a self-approved life in harmony with the Universe where we claim our Divine birthright to create our best life.

We all drift into confusion and we've all had experiences of dualistic thinking as we journey through life. We also have an amazing gift and the capacity to realign ourselves with clarity. There are essentially two parts of knowledge. The first comes from intellectual learning through studies, books, workshops, etc., and the second one is a knowing through our direct experiences with life. Wisdom comes from the second. I feel that knowledge comes from the other side of our ability to sit with two things at once that both appear to be true. Whereby conflict is the tension we feel when we have two mutually exclusive choices. The tension of seeming opposites seems to reveal the illusion of separation. This happens when there are incongruences between our thinking mind and our loving heart. Processing our thinking through the heart helps us to see the illusion of our thoughts, offering us guidance to the living truth, within our heart.

It is this experiential wisdom where we meet ourselves. Our

experiences are the mirror of life that paves the way to heal our own wounds and the wounds of others. While delving into the stories we created, or by listening to the stories of others, we find that we are able to draw from a compassionate knowing, enabling us to offer our self and others something that might be constructive—even if is simply friendship.

By remaining in the space in which all things are true, where there is no separation, we find ourselves in the midst of a higher truth. The practice of sitting with "not knowing" begins with trust in the unnamable mysterious space that holds us all. This is the vast space of knowledge leading to wisdom. It is a place where we all meet our self and each other in the safety of this sacred space. It is in the brilliant light of this space, we learn to deepen our commitment and our trust in ourselves, in each other, and in life itself.

We need to practice feeling comfortable with the tension of opposites and to practice our ability to accept "not knowing." The practice is to feel with the heart, deeper beneath the illusion. When things are unclear, not obvious, or the tension between right and wrong is mired by judgment, assumptions, old beliefs, etc., our job is to wait and to endure the tensions. As uncomfortable as this feels sometimes, it requires a crucial ongoing practice to not act prematurely by naming or labeling what we encounter in our experiences. The truth requires us not to make assumptions, opinions, or beliefs in haste. Take the time required for the truth to reveal itself; to surround us fully as we journey within the threshold of transformation.

The Greek word para (beyond) and dox (belief) is more than simply a paradox of "beyond belief." It feels more like beyond our current understanding of things. Without the courage and patience to feel beneath the surface of our experiences, and without the ability to trust the waiting process, we are not able to grasp the transformational gifts that come to us from Not Knowing.

If we are restless, constantly moving from place to place, job to job, or relationship to relationship, the foundation is both weak and undefined. We will not have strong boundaries to hold our Life Force Energy and this creates restlessness and a constant desire for change. Patience is a defining quality of our foundation. It allows us to firmly and fully root ourselves into life. We can only be truly creative and happy when we are rooted in our own life.

We all want to feel secure in our lives, but what many of us perceive as security does not exist. True security is not found in the outer material world, nor is it found in our relationships with others. In fact, true and lasting security does not come from anything exterior to our being. It is inner security that regulates us and gives us a sense of well-being. It is an absolute knowing that we are a part of the whole that allows us to let down our guard, relax, and recharge our Life Force Energy. It is inner security we need to cultivate and this is our connection to our Divine Source. When we have this peace within, it releases us from fear and worry about our survival. Ultimately, it helps us create reserves of our Life Force Energy for going through challenging times.

We need only experience this inner security in order to feel protected in all aspects of life. Inner security lets us thrive, and in doing so, we come to know the truth and beauty of our spirit. Inner security helps us to remain focused on the good in our lives and lets us define healthy boundaries that provide a margin for comfort, ease, and assurance. Security attached to something exterior is usually an illusion. It is stability that keeps us steady through change. Stability implies being balanced and having the ability to be flexible and to move with the flow of life. It stops us from becoming reactive or feeling threatened. Stability allows us to focus on our inner world. It supports our Awareness and gives us a clear perception of the world around us. When we learn to live from our center, we know what is best for us, how to readjust ourselves to remain steady and constant, and how to trust in life.

The journey into self can be a time for each of us to strive to be entirely and completely one with self; patient with self; accepting all aspects of self, and simply enjoying life fully. Expect and allow miracles and synchronicity to show up in the most amazing ways during the discovery process and in the most intelligent way, may you realize that you are one with all that is.

DS: Indeed, dear friend, you have outlined the great benefits of living free from the old paradigm of security's superstition. We all must realize that there is no such thing as security. A long time ago security existed only in Paradise; but living in today's world requires that we develop the willingness to let go of securities; break down the emotional prison walls and allow our heart's courage and determination to embrace all possibilities. We must remember not to act like an oyster that closes to protect its pearl, but let our soul shine instead. We must keep searching for life's beauty and grace, keep moving ahead, and choose to open the door to our own destiny.

Christina, you have said our mind attaches easily to outside sources and keeps craving for more knowledge. Many times, I have wondered what it is that makes one's mind to love life like heaven and another to live a life akin to hell. One body to dance with the Universe, while the other resisting change to stand still and let the life clock run out. I believe that the answer is Awareness and understanding the interplay between mind-heart, between beliefs, thoughts, and emotions.

We need to balance our emotions by witnessing our thoughts and discover our belief systems, which cause our feelings in order to transform them to right thinking and right action through the power of our will. We must learn to shift our attention from the mind that has a tendency to create vibrations of lower energy to our heart and align our self to our higher Life Force Energy frequencies.

We must learn to believe that our heart holds eternal beauty and mystery and resonates with all the surroundings. Our heart's cosmic and loving capacities can embrace all life and cosmos. The seat of wisdom is in our loving heart that offers us the fulfillment between earthly and cosmic forces.

We must realize that we are never separate from each other and that while we live in the Universe, the Universe is also always within us. Spirit lives everywhere and we are one in spirit. Our spiritual body detects the workings of Spirit and we all have within us an inner living light of primordial, ever-present, non-dual Awareness that lights up our whole of creation.

When we start to become aware of our thoughts, we connect with our natural state of mind. Think of yourself walking down on a lovely beach, while you are aware where you are. At the same time, you are being contained by the elements of fire (sun) water, air and earth, and if you allow yourself to see everything for the first time, then that moment becomes complete Awareness and Aliveness.

When we are open to what is happening and at the same time contained, then we have no more pre-conceived notions and through the pathway of Awareness, we are able to experience things with an open heart. Understanding the workings of the mind and heart is extremely important. While our heart feels, our mind thinks. Our heart is actually the inner organ of perception and as such, it is the means by which the head perceives everything that takes place in the body.

The Universe, with its living wisdom, maintains unity in all cosmic relationships. Now, more than ever, through the use of Emotional Intelligence, Awareness and our imagination, we can gain access to the Universe's pure energy, laws of vibration, intelligence and unconditional love. We are all Universal higher-level beings and can transcend our mind to unify all. We are all strong vessels that carry the celestial forces of wisdom, agape, passion, and discernment for truth.

We must stop identifying with our body, our feelings, and thoughts and instead start to transform our self-importance and self-reflection and move away from the illusion of being separate. Our innate sense of growth potential is only limited by our imagination and our intimations of a higher state of being are true. The Universe has a remarkable plan for us and through its cosmic love and energy we become conscious partners with God.

CR: Yes, Dimitrios, we must not close the door. We must instead keep moving toward our destiny. It is essential to maintain balance for creating a firm foundation in our life. Our heart contracts in pain and opens and expands with pleasure and it requires a balance to maintain a healthy flow. We need clarity and presence to think about how we are going to implement our next best right action steps and goals so we can achieve success and happiness. We want and need a sharp mind to see us through life's decisions. The power of learning right thinking takes a combination of detachment and wisdom to guide us in making wholesome choices for creating our best life. The power of these attributes is in being able to discern, gather knowledge, and distill wisdom and access intuitive knowing.

When we are lost in our emotions, we are unable to experience fully our present environment. Are we preventing our own joy? For example, are we setting any particular conditions, such as attachments or expectations, for what constitutes happiness? And if these self-imposed conditions are not fulfilled, is it also possible that we might be refusing to feel happiness? Many of our emotions can distance us from our happiness and we will never find the answers or solutions to the experiences we find ourselves in solely with logic. If we want to experience the joyful divinity of every present moment, we will need to let go of any beliefs that limit and distort it and we must work cooperatively with mind and heart.

As you have said, the biggest obstacle to that experience is the illusory feeling of separateness created by our senses, when in fact we are one spirit, one with all energy, and even one with all matter. This feeling of being separate from others and the forces around us causes us to fear and develop defense mechanisms that seriously obstruct our happiness. Life becomes easier if we develop our capacity to stay in Awareness of the present experience and see ourselves as loving consciousness finding solutions that benefit all rather than see ourselves as self-serving and others as separate bodies and minds.

Accepting things and others as they are, we can learn to take responsibility for all of our experiences and even for all those we see as problems. "Our only responsibility is our response-ability." Taking responsibility means not blaming anyone or anything for our situation, for our feelings, for the attachments, or the expected outcome we have, and this includes our self. Every problem is an opportunity in disguise, alerting us to opportunities that allow us to take each experience in each present moment and transform it into a greater benefit for the good of the whole. Using our Awareness, we can relinquish the need to defend our point of view, and we will feel no need to persuade others to accept our point of view. Instead, we allow others to be who they are and we remain open to all points of view without becoming rigidly attached to any one of them.

Committing our self to detachment allows our self, and those around us, the freedom to be as they are and not rigidly impose our ideas of how things should be. We are not forcing solutions on problems, which sometimes even creates new problems. Instead, we participate in everything with detached involvement. Factoring in uncertainty in any of our situations as an essential ingredient of our experiences, coupled with our willingness to accept uncertainty, often creates surprising solutions that spontaneously emerge out of the problem, out of the confusion, disorder, and chaos. The more uncertain things seem to be, the more secure we will feel, because uncertainty is our path to freedom. Through the wisdom of uncertainty, we will find our security.

Dimitrios, as you said earlier, we need to follow the patterns of nature realizing that our sorry attempts to separate and pull apart what the mind cannot understand or a heart that feels numbness or indifference is a spiritual disability. In each century it seems we take turns being the caretaker of our beautiful Earth, and we need to take responsibility for the seeds we have sown in the name of Humanity for the next generation. Seems in each generation we take turns pondering when things might fall apart and seek to discover the mystery beneath all that falls apart. The Universe is organized beyond our comprehension, and it is important for us to explore our own humanness and our place in this world. Each of us must continue to access without any real certainty which way the Universe appears to be unfolding. Is it breaking apart, coming together, or is it a tangled weave of both?

Nature continues to germinate itself with ease. It just is what it is and does what it does. The wisdom is within the seed. Those that fall onto hard rock don't even get a chance to sprout. Others fall among bushes and sprout, but soon die as they are unable to get enough sunlight to develop. Those that fall onto good earth develop and produce fruit. Many seeds of wisdom fall into the field of our mind. How many of them actually sprout and grow and bear fruit in our daily lives?

The path of wisdom is understanding, discrimination, and philosophy. It's a path that many of us find ourselves on and it takes razor sharp, spiritual discrimination—always aware of the truth that we are not the contents of the mind, or the body, and that everything we see is just a temporary reality. A reality that is always changing and will soon pass.

Earlier we spoke about Emotional Intelligence, everyone has some, and when faced with any experience, we have only a few seconds to respond before the subconscious mind hijacks the conscious mind. This is a biological function of how the mind works. I began this practice by noticing when I felt triggered by an experience or a memory of an experience. First, remember it's a CYCLE. We might not have the perfect Awareness to identify the exact right choice, but as we go around and around this process, it gets easier!

There are three parts to understand about this process and we go deeper into the process in the self-help section at the end of the chapter. The three parts consist of the following:

Know Yourself—This is the "what." When you Know Yourself, you know your strengths and challenges. You know what you are doing; what you want; and what you want to change. Everyone has feelings all the time. What are yours? Not just the obvious ones, but the ones hiding in the background. Remember that emotions are data. They're chemical signals to help us handle threats and opportunities.

Choose Your Highest Self—this provides the "how." It shows you how to take action. It also shows you how to influence yourself and others and how to "operationalize" concepts. When a situation just starts to heat up, "press the pause button." Take a big breath. Get water. Say, "Let me think about this for a moment." Or perhaps simply explain that you need a moment to process what is happening. There are very few situations that actually require an instant reaction. Remember you have many options. Sometimes it's hard to see those. You can change your thoughts, engage new feelings, and experiment with new actions. You might not have "the perfect solution," but you do have possibilities.

Give Yourself—delivers the "why." When you give yourself, you are clear and full of energy so you stay focused. It provides the why to respond a certain way, or why to move in a new direction, and why others might want to join you in reaching a solution or conclusion that benefits all. There's always more to the story. When people do or say something annoying, get curious. Ask the following: What's really going on here? Your choices matter. The way you respond affects others and affects you. It will affect the future. What's the effect you want to have?

This cycle must begin within seconds of being triggered and before falling into the pit of overwhelming emotions. If we have fallen into the overwhelm pit, then the point of making a difference in the present moment has passed and we will need to wait it out until we, or the other parties involved, come out of their struggle with their emotions. In other words, we will need to choose another time to work through the experience because the mind has already been hijacked by the emotions. Doing this process consistently is a challenge. Practicing will perfect it to a point in time whereby you will learn to live from the place of Awareness.

If we use the Awareness practice we spoke of earlier, and we are not in overwhelm, then the first thing we need to do is step back from the experience into a place where we become the observer of the experience. From this space of Awareness, you will be able to see the three parts of every experience—you the observer, the experience or issue, and how the experience is being processed.

As followers of this path, we gradually cease to identify with the body, emotions, and contents of the mind. We begin to experience our Self as the "WITNESS" of all these changing phenomena that are taking place all around us. Before we were born, the drama did not exist. During our life in the physical body, we are in a dream like state—the power of the illusion of the material world. We experience the drama of our human incarnation in all its physical variations. We simply have a role to play and sometimes we become lost in the role.

Then one day the curtain will fall. The dream will end. The "I" will find that it has been sitting in the audience witnessing the dramas all this time. When the reality of the witness is remembered, one experiences the nature of the REAL, or the truth of one's eternal, unchanging nature. One experiences pure unmodified consciousness and eternal bliss based on no external or changing phenomena. We all have the capacity to create happy and joyful lives and we do this by allowing and accepting all that is and by participating in the excitement that can occur when we remain an observer—open to the infinity of choices as we step into the field of all possibilities. We then fully experience all the fun, adventure, magic, and mystery of life. We all experience eternal existence, pure unmodified consciousness, and eternal bliss. We all come to know that these three qualities are totally unaffected and undisturbed by the changing flow of events and experiences occurring in the dream drama of life.

*

Going Deeper

CR: At the point when we have beaten the six seconds we are in Awareness and now we need to feel things fully, tune in and notice our feelings and reactions. Now get off autopilot. In other words, use your willpower and control. Do not jump into the experience with habitual behavior. This step is Know Yourself.

Through the curious and wondrous process of self-discovery, we often stumble beautifully into the spaces between our thoughts and our suffering. Living in Awareness challenges us to see everything from a higher perspective, discovering the truth that holds us all, daring us to mix the elements of our heart and mind making all things visible. All of us are here to help unravel each other and to make our way back to love through the mirror of life.

Take some time to reflect upon a current experience you are challenged with.

Now take a moment to reflect on your comfort level with not knowing any particular outcome.

What does your living presence say to you? Ask yourself how can you move closer to it?

How comfortable are you with feeling into and internalizing your experiences?

Are you able to let go of your internal argument with your experiences or with life?

Can you trust the underlying wholeness of life that waits beneath your arguments?

Journaling

CR: Now that you are off autopilot and living in this place of Awareness instead of reacting, give yourself a moment to de-escalate and evaluate your options. Observe yourself and the others in the experience. See if you can see the bigger issue. Notice the triggers, yours and the others, and take action using words of compassion to de-escalate the emotions and the angst of the experience. This step is Choose Your Highest Self.

Listening to your heart, I invite you to journal about a question you are currently carrying. Call to this question honestly so it might open a door in your life right now. From a place of Awareness, see yourself below the illusion in the wonderful gritty nature of things as they are by listening, translating, and questioning your experience. Which part of you opened the door? Ask yourself was it your active listener—your deep speaker—or your seeker of the truth. Which of these is the most experienced within you and which needs more of your attention?

Connect with Others

CR: Now go ahead and connect with the others in the experience. Remember what's truly important to you. Have consideration of the others and move forward with those in mind. Remember that we have all been programmed by well-meaning others and people do what they do, say what they say, based on this programming. Hold a loving space for yourself and the others as you find your way through the experience and back to love. This step is Giving Yourself.

It's really simple. Practice by taking a few seconds a few times a day to go through those steps. You can use these three questions: What am I feeling? What options do I have? What do I really want?

Start a conversation with a friend or loved one sharing the experience and your insights from your journaling. Tell the story of your experience, not from a victim's point of view, but by way of an example of that small part of your life. Share how your experience opened up a larger sense of life simply by giving it your attention. Discuss your experience and what insights or questions surfaced for you.

Milestones

CR: When we listen with our heart, we allow the reality of things to touch us beneath the surface of our identity. When we are authentic and real, we come closer to what matters and the questioning and listening draws us away from our familiar habitual logic into the realm of perspective, a view of reality and eternity. Celebrate the milestones of courage it takes to sit still with patience in the not knowing or the courage to say what you see in your discovery process through your own inner vision. This is how the soul opens the door so we can begin to make sense of our experiences in life.

The Mind is the Map

PART I: THE PROCESS

By learning to Live Lightly we can become and act as a radiant beacon of light for ourselves and our world. We begin to cultivate a highly-refined Life Force Energy field within us and around us—a field that carries all the dimensions of life within it. The source of our power is the organizing principle central to civilization and emanates from pure consciousness.

FINDING JOY

X

Learning to Live Lightly

PART II:

CULTIVATING THE JOURNEY

*"Happiness blooms naturally in the hearts of those
who are inwardly free. It flows spontaneously,
like a mountain spring after April showers, in
minds that are contented with simple living."*

- Paramahansa Yogananda

CHAPTER TEN

LEARNING TO LIVE LIGHTLY

CR: WHAT DOES it mean to Live Lightly? I'll begin here with a simple definition of Lightly. It means with little weight or force—without care or concern—in a way that is not serious—in a quick and graceful way. I learned to Live Lightly while on sabbatical in Greece for two years. However, we could be anywhere on this wonderful planet of ours, perhaps on a mountain or by the sea. We might feast on the canopy of the blue sky and puffy white clouds or look at the waves cresting and falling back on the water. We might take in the incredible views from the mountaintop, but if we try to contain or grasp these wonders, we will only be grabbing at the air. However, if we try to push them away, we will find they do not resist.

Living Lightly happens when we SLOW DOWN. It happens when we realize the best way to seize our human essence is to realize that there is nothing to grasp. It is the pulling and pushing in life that causes so much suffering, our own, and that of others. Living Lightly means we STOP doing that. We let go of the pushing and pulling of energy and feel the essence of the void—the emptiness—and then we fulfill the purpose of our human life. By experiencing the beauty around us, feel how easy it is to slip into total serenity and bliss. Live this essence, share this essence, and we will be able to bring others along with us to experience through our example, increasing their Life Force Energy as well.

To Live Lightly, we must learn to live in the present moment and to accept things as they are. We need to live within that framework mindfully. Live in the wonder of it all and develop a strong curiosity of self. No longer expect good or bad things to happen; simply take in life as it happens and be content with whatever comes. Begin by observing and becoming more aware of your thoughts and feelings. Notice any judgments coming up. Notice if you have any attachments or expectations. Over time, we might find ourselves paying witness to this more and more and we will become conscious of these thoughts. When we STOP judging things as good or bad, we are free from the burdens of the emotion of judgment, and can live lighter, freer. Without the human mind, things just happen, and they are not good or bad. It's only when we apply the filter of our judgment that they become good or bad, beautiful or ugly. Therefore, another aspect of Living Lightly is the importance of dropping expectations—not just lowering them—but eliminating them!

By Living Lightly, we learn to live in perfect grace with an absolute knowing all is as it is and all is always perfect for our evolution to higher states of being human. In this interconnected Universe, every improvement we made on an individual level in our private worlds improves the world at large for everyone. It is through this that we all float on the collective level of consciousness of mankind so that any increment we add to the collective echoes back to us. We all add to our common buoyancy by our efforts to benefit all life.

Many times, on my journey others asked me if I was a seeker. I recall the first time I was asked this question. I remained quiet for a few moments feeling into the question. I could remember a time in my life that I did feel this way, when I felt like a seeker. Life was not working well for me. The quality of my life had not been good, or at least it was not what I expected, and I spent a lot of my alone time trying to figure out what was wrong with my life and ways to fix it. I felt like I was pushing and pulling my way through life, rather than just living my life from a place of freedom and joy.

I had bookcases full of self-help material written by others. I attended many workshops, seminars and classes, and indeed I felt like a spiritual vagabond. Although I was gaining lots of knowledge, I gained nothing in the way of experiential wisdom that would initiate change. I came to realize that change happens from the inside and I had lots of work to do. I glanced over at the twelve boxes full of my personal journals I had shipped to Greece for the purpose of going deeper. I put them in date order and began my inner journey. Revisiting them poked my heart—no it was more like stabbing at my heart. I discovered I had so much programming, so many needs, so many attachments, so many incomplete experiences, and so many more experiences I needed to let go of. The original question became the bigger question. I asked myself, a seeker of what?

Instead of seeking outside our self, we need to go directly to the source and realize who we are as a being in the co-creation of our own life. Seeking is a word often applied to the spiritual path, and many people are proud to call themselves seekers. Often people continue to seek with an addictive intensity seeking with a new hope to find God—the soul or the higher self. The problem here is that seeking begins with this false assumption. The manner of seeking is doomed because it is a chase that takes one outside of self.

When I began my real work of inner self-realization and discovery, I learned, experientially, that one of the most important aspects of healing self is our willingness to accept all the parts of our self. This means the aspects we like and the aspects we fear. We will need to face and accept even our own shadow side. These are the feelings and parts of ourselves that we have rejected, repressed, or disowned. All of this work is done in Awareness. It is inner work, not the seeking of anything external to our being.

Productive seeking requires that we throw out all assumptions that there is a prize to be won. This means acting without an attachment to the outcome of rising to some ideal self. Hoping or wishing that you will get somewhere better than the place you started from. We are starting from our self, wherever we are in the present moment, and it is that self that contains all the answers. So, we must give up on the idea that we must go from one place to another. In fact, there is no linear path when the goal isn't somewhere else. We must discard any fixed judgments about high and low, good and evil, holy and profane. There is only one reality and that reality contains everything in its tangle of experiences. What we are really trying to find is the experiencer who is present no matter what the experience might be.

We need to make a continuous effort towards self-discovery, self-improvement, and spiritual growth and this requires inner work. Making these efforts brings us many successes such as health, vitality, a more positive and effective mind, greater creativity, and many other benefits. It is good to remember that even while doing this work, we will still be identified with the Ego and still living in the ignorance of our programmed minds. We might feel as though we are living a happier and more positive life, but we are not free of the Ego. In fact, the Ego will never be enlightened because enlightenment is simply the realization that we are not the Ego—that we are not the body and the mind. Our personality will never be enlightened. We will simply stop identifying with the personality and become the unlimited observer and essence—a witness of all. Of course, the personality can be greatly improved but the perfection of Divine virtues can come only when we are no longer identified with the body and mind and their fears.

Somewhere along the way someone coined the phrase "spiritual materialism" trying to model and transfer the values that work in the material world over to the spiritual world. My feeling is that there are pitfalls associated with knowing where you are going and struggling to get there, often using someone else's map. It is better to remain in the not knowing. Spiritual growth is spontaneous and both the big and small events come along unexpectedly. A single word can open your heart. A single glance can tell you who you really are. Awakening doesn't happen according to some plan. Don't struggle to get there. None of our plans and goals can prepare us for the moment when we ripen. What we can do is try not to define ourselves by all the layers covering us. When we are ripe within, our soul fills out like a mature peach and once ripened, we are able to feel compassion and joy underneath the soft warm fuzzy covering of the stories we tell ourselves, for nothing matters to the peach except the sweetness within. There comes a moment when our endless dreams and goals have served their purpose. It will be a time when we have experienced the cave or the solstice and solitude of a long journey. And just like the peach, we realize that we are full enough. We will feel a rejuvenated sweetness that has incubated within us, like the sun rays bursting and propelling us forward into a new understanding of our self. In the ripeness of renewal, we will find that we have set ourselves free in the mist of this great change.

Although self-improvement is real, and it does help, don't make the spiritual path a self-improvement project. We don't need to get there. In other words, we do our inner work, but don't get stuck in the mire. It takes a strong sense of self to confront the many obstacles and challenges on the path. Expanded Awareness comes at a price. We will have to give up our limitations and sometimes our feelings of being victimized as these limitations will slow down the spiritual progress. The wise thing to do is to seek help at the level where the problem exists by confronting the shadow energies within.

I've met many people who give up on spirituality because they felt it wasn't working for them or it didn't happen fast enough. The best way to avoid this pitfall is not to set a timetable. Simply allow the process to unfold while giving support to our self in the process of spiritual growth. Don't wait for a miracle. There is only one reality. Our task is to break through boundaries of division and separation. Watching for and waiting for a miracle keeps the boundaries in place. There is no separation, there never was. There is only one Unity of all there is.

We need to realize that we are not the Ego. It is the Ego that is seeking, however, we can see through the false sense of identifying with the Ego, but that realization is experiential and not intellectual. We will need to pass through the physics class of non-duality. It is from this understanding that we will know that we are not an object-observer or experiencer. While this knowledge might temporarily satisfy the mind, the heart still longs for more. It remains unsatisfied. We cannot read, hear, watch, or think our way to the experience of spirituality. However powerfully evocative, these will only bring us to the frontiers of our personal process of discovery. We cannot come to the experience by reading a description, however profound and articulate, or looking at photos, however beautiful. Pure Awareness is only experienced when all that appears ceases, including the experiencer-perceiver. We will need to remember to remind our self and re-concluding, again and again, the concept that, "All there is—is One Consciousness."

Seeking can't get anyone out of the tangle because EVERYTHING is tangled up, everything is ONE. The only thing that will ever be pure and pristine is our own Awareness and the mystery of it all. As our Awareness grows, the opposites, the separation, and division begin to calm down and something else emerges—a world we will feel at home in. Awareness offers an alternative beyond the fray. It is a place where we meet our self and we will be able to create anything in existence.

The "I AM" contains all that is needed for making a world, even though by itself it consists of nothing but a silent witness.

DS: Thank you, Christina for the great guidance of Living Lightly. Just like you said, we don't need to follow someone else's map and simply enough, work on our own virtues and values. Learning to Live Lightly allows us to orient our thinking towards the true, our feelings towards the beautiful, and our will towards the Good.

We can connect to our higher nature, our own I AM, and be truly astonished in our seeking. Seeking is just like devotion, an active force. It's a mercurial quality. Our Soul is filled with Fire and when we seek connection with the spiritual worlds, we need to be like an alchemist, a master of fire, finding and connecting to our own inner sacred fire.

Understanding the workings of the mind and heart can teach us how to Live Lightly. And as we have said previously, while our heart feels, our mind thinks. Our heart is actually the inner organ of perception by means of which the head perceives everything that takes place in the body. When our mind sees a flower, it sees it in black and white, while our heart sees it in three dimensions and senses its color, beauty, and warmth. The heart feels the interiority of things and moves in the world with a sense of not-knowing and first-time discovery. Once our spiritual eyes open up, we will be able to see in people quite remarkable aspects, different than the normal aspects we see with our normal eyes.

CR: Yes, and once we have identified this, we begin to favor the subtleness and value of this level of Awareness as it grows in the infinite diversity of creation. The way we perceive the world within us and around us gives rise to how we chose to live in our world and mirrors that back to us as our personal reality.

Our imagination always has another card to play in the unfolding of our lives. Even one small thought about the beauty and goodness all around us can create a tiny sensation, which triggers a whole new pattern to emerge. When this happens, one has found the path of expanded Awareness. And if one pursues this momentary glimpse of Awareness, one will feel it expand and this single thread can often lead to a complex tapestry to our higher self or higher essence.

While this metaphor cannot explain how to change reality itself, to master this pure Awareness one must learn to live it. That essence is that love of God, selfless action, and knowledge are trying to teach. It is only illusion that masks the greater "I" that exists in everyone. Our real identity, pure and simple is the "I AM" of all that exists. And all of us share the same "I AM." Fulfillment in life occurs when our being is able to embrace this so much that God is also included in our sense of being alive. Unity is a state that is attainable and as Dimitrios said above, we need to become like an alchemist reaching the state where nothing is left out of the "I AM."

We are all one. To actually feel this oneness, we only need live from a place of Awareness. For example, it's as if one was walking down a street and sees a complete stranger. Your eyes meet and for some reason there is a connection. Not of a sexual, romantic or of a suspicious nature, but indeed more of an epiphany. The epiphany being that you are that stranger and your experience merges with his. Call it a feeling or a thought—it doesn't matter—it's the sudden expansion that counts. One seemingly gets flung outside our narrow boundaries and if only for a moment, one has tasted a hidden dimension beyond the walls of the Ego and one feels lighter, freer, even happier. As you said, this is realizing we are all embedded into the world of spirit.

DS: We also need to keep in mind and heart that we have a spiritual gift and that is our thinking, not our thoughts. Our thinking process is a spiritual gift—a living force that arranges concepts together and like you have previously said, makes us aware. Our imagination will connect us to Universal spiritual concepts and the Spiritual worlds. In addition, our heart is a holy vessel of sacred purity—a receptivity that illuminates our world with holiness.

CR: Yes, I feel that higher-level thinking will point the way whenever our mind stops being restless and speculative. On this path, it is better to pay attention to our inner voice for the purpose of self-discovery and transformation than any attempts to silence our internal dialogue. For example, we want to know what the voice is saying because it is a clue to what's written on our wall. Our inner work will transform our thinking into experiential knowledge, which is to say wisdom. Eventually, with practice, our mind will not feel so driven, and a new sense of clarity and stillness will emerge enabling us to look at a problem and actually only see solutions. Then, using the power of our imagination, we can take consciousness one step further into creation and reality. I personally have found that as knowingness expands personal questions actually fade. Perhaps what the mind really wants is to know the mystery of existence.

DS: To invest inward.

CR: Yes. Nothing can happen that is outside of the one reality and yes, my friend, the journey is inward. The investment is learning to relate to Awareness itself, the purest level of experience.

As we develop internal Awareness, we can be assured that we can become and act as a radiant beacon of light for ourselves and our world. We begin to cultivate a highly-refined Life Force Energy field within us and around us—a field that carries the spiritual dimensions of our life within it. The source of our power is inarguable and in itself it is the organizing principle central to civilization and emanates from pure consciousness. It is a visible manifestation of the invisible and we can help raise the energetic vibration of our Universe to one of unconditional love for all. We must understand that nothing is hidden and truth stands everywhere revealed to everyone. It has to do with values, motive and principle, and it is always associated with that which supports the significance of life itself. This power uplifts, dignifies, and ennobles and requires no justification. This power doesn't move against anything at all—it remains still, total, and complete within itself and requires nothing from the outside. It makes no demands and it has no needs.

There are aspects of the Divine presence living within us that carry the power of reconciliation, healing and grace for our lives. When we awaken and are living the path of Spirit, we can see how we have been guided through many circumstances, and many people, to take the next step on our path with a spiritual consciousness of our own life as well as understanding of the circumstances and choices others made as well. At this point we are open to receive direct guidance from the angelic realm—the Christ Light and the Holy Spirit, and the mystery of life unfolds before us as we follow a path of light, and wonder, knowing all is well.

Living Lightly in this way we are building and containing all the Life Force Energy we need to live a conscious, happy, and intentional life. It is a life whereby we understand that it is sustained by our indelible link to God as our Source. It is the link to spirit through our prayers, petitions, visions, and hopes at the level that we know all that we need is provided for us and that we are blessed in endless ways that fulfill our best life.

*

Going Deeper

CR: A big part of Emotional Intelligence is the continuance to evolve to a greater sense of Awareness—to continue to grow ourselves—to hold a loving space for others and for society as a whole as we evolve together as One. Sometimes if we become absorbed in such efforts we might naturally also become attached to our specific ideas of success and when we do not, or until we do achieve what we consider our success, we might feel some frustration often resulting in rejecting ourselves, others, and society. We might feel inferior because we have not yet succeeded or we feel whatever we are doing is not making a difference. Becoming attached to any result, inner or outer, for ourselves or others, is a major source of anxiety, tension, and conflict within ourselves and with others. While we do need to make an effort, we also need to learn to accept ourselves and others at each stage of our growth exactly as we are and also to accept our life situation as it is until we are able to change it.

Sometimes we may feel we have stopped growing. We're not interested in improving our self and, thus, may become complacent about how life, society, or the world is showing up from our perspective. There is a tendency towards isolation and to shut out the outer and inner worlds preferring to remain living the way we always have been even if this is unpleasant and painful. Some people prefer a world that has become familiar rather than subject themselves to change and embrace the unknown even though the unknown may hold the promise of greater happiness, peace, and love. In my own process of personal growth, I knew that I needed to make more of an effort towards transformation and accept that the Divine design of evolution will not allow us to simply rest. We can ignore it for periods of time, but sooner or later the life events and situations happening around us will force us to awaken and we will need to accept change and transformation to emerge like a butterfly from its cocoon. Everything that exists is pure energy and change and evolution is the stuff our entire Universe is made of.

Staying with what matters involves setting down our opinions and preconceptions of how we would like things to be and living directly into life as it is. Our work here is one of a discovery process and one of trusting your intuition. It is the work of learning to live your inborn nature as it relates to everything, and to know you are a beautiful spark in the all of Divine creation.

Check in now with your breath. How often do you hold your breath?

What will it take for you to breathe deeply—emptying and opening your practice of staying in Awareness?

Are you accepting the experience before you right now? Or are you resisting any aspects?

Are you allowing an injury, wound, or any perceived limitation to hold you back from living fully in life?

Who is the one within you that says yes, and who is the one within you that says no? Listen to the mind chatter and try to hear all that is said and even what is unsaid. What might you be pretending not to hear or know?

Can you open to the soft moment in your center? Can you endure the pain of uncertainty until it shows you another deeper way?

What old way of being or seeing can you let go of that will return you to the freshness of now?

Journaling

CR: Journaling helps us with the work of being and in keeping things real. I invite you to write in your journal each day. Re-read and update it often as your discovery process moves you along to new insights. By personalizing your conversation within your writings, you can explore even deeper as this becomes the living connection of all that is within you and all that holds the history of the presence and wisdom of your highest self. Let go of trying to control the mind in your journal. One way to do that is to write with your non-dominant hand. While it may appear a bit messy, you will be surprised at what comes forth when we drop the controlling.

Write a journal entry about an experience you are having that is causing you to lose your sense of connection to others or your feelings of peace and wellbeing. Be sure to include what you might believe that is causing any disturbances towards your ability to feel peace and wellbeing. Try to capture all the emotions that come up for you when you think about cultivating peace and wellbeing in your life.

Connect with Others

CR: There is a "higher love" that is present in the Universal Life Force Energy and this love is not the ordinary love of this world. This love is the center of all life. The heart is the center of our Life Force Energy. It radiates from our heart, which is the sacred chamber of love, and the temple of the Divine presence within us. It is the truth of our being and the conduit for love to flow through us. It never forgets an act of kindness or a moment of love and stores the memories of love deep within its hidden chambers. It is forgiveness that sets the heart free from the bondage of anger, hate or enmity, and as we heal the wounds of the heart, we release and forgive so we can return to our natural state of love.

We create our best life and increase the flow of our Life Force Energy as we free ourselves from emotional pain and forgive hurt allowing the universal energy of love to flow as the mighty river it is. To live our best life, we must feel the flow of universal love to be fulfilled no matter how that is expressed. Love recognizes itself only in love.

By choosing this Divine love and opening our hearts, it becomes our way of living. It will keep our spirit strong. As we create the intention to claim this love, it becomes easier to allow it into our being—to embrace the wonder of love and to become aware of the times we feel separate from the source of love. At those moments, we must accept and allow life to bring us new experiences of the miracles of love in our ordinary daily life. Asking the simple question, "What would love do now?" empowers and encourages us to cultivate a belief in ease and to trust a higher spiritual wisdom for the experiences we have and also to assist us to be clear about our choices for love.

Spiritual consciousness is dependent on us accessing Unconditional Love. Once we have anchored and integrated it, we interface with the world from a place of empowerment and compassion. We must work to expand our self-worth, enhance our self-respect, and honor the Soul within us. We work to develop a greater sense of self-esteem that enables us to claim our freedom of choice. We must express the choices that define us and to honor our personality as the individual manifestation of our light. What we like, desire and choose are reflections of our individual choices that help carry us through the emotional and spiritual initiations that make us strong, resilient, and more conscious individuals. This teaches us who we are at a foundational level. No one can diminish this foundation because it is the rock that illuminates our world.

Start a conversation with a friend or loved one sharing the experience and your insights from your journaling. Start by feeling into what's real for you and opening a discussion of the current state of your being with regards to aspects of you in your present moment. It is important to remember that whatever is within our experience is never about the other person or anything external to us.

Discuss the current state of your heart and how it functions. Does it function from pain, fear, worry, anxiety or does it function from love, peace, and unity? Which comes naturally? Which is most challenging? Now considering how your heart functions, in what ways would you like to grow?

Milestones

CR: Reflecting back on life through my journals, I noticed I seldom, if ever, wrote about the successes or milestones I accomplished. I sat there thinking about my accomplishments. This turned to thinking about personal limits I had to deal or come to terms with. I was beginning to understand my patterns on a deeper level and this reflection was expanding my perspective, having greater empathy for myself and others than when I first recorded the events. I found myself examining issues, which might have prevented me from fulfilling my potential. In order to avoid repeating the same patterns, I had to acknowledge them. One new question came to mind in that process. That question was, "What do I feel about me right now?" I thought about the life I really wanted to create, instead of the one I thought I should live. Once again, I felt perhaps the "should" was someone else's idea. I started getting clear about what I wanted and I worked to change my beliefs and replace the habits I had created with more effective, empowering ones. My past experiences were the most helpful tools for learning about myself. I was able to see how certain choices, behaviors, and circumstances had led me to where I was currently. What I realized was that the most effective way to improve my life was often counter-intuitive—against conventional wisdom and what I had been taught.

To enter the unknown and even the unspeakable requires a soft courage and patience, waiting until the urging voices of our mind has nothing more to shout about and until there is nothing more to reach for and nothing left to let go of. Take note of all the times in your life you have opened your heart until what you could not see or hear was received and felt internally and thoroughly enough to initiate change, altering the way in which you live in the world. Reflect on all the times you were able to accept your experiences and able to sit in stillness with enough patience and silence to allow this change to happen. Record and celebrate these milestones along your journey. Each one of them reveals the path ahead and each one contains a promise of Living Lightly.

The Mind is the Map

PART I: THE PROCESS

Passion comes from our heart and is our greatest motivator in all areas of life, relationships, work, hobbies, etc. Choose to live your life on purpose and to show up for life with great passion to joyfully create your unique life experiences. When living life passionately, you get to witness the fruits of your intentions and transform your dreams into reality. This is bliss. This is passion!

FINDING JOY

XI

Living Life with Passion

PART II:

CULTIVATING THE JOURNEY

"When it's over, I want to say all my life —
I was a bride married to amazement.
I was the bridegroom, taking the world into my arms"

- Mary Oliver

CHAPTER ELEVEN

LIVING LIFE WITH PASSION

C R: WE HAVE all together, as humanity, created and chosen this life and our experiences as opportunities to take our next step towards freedom from fear and the illusion of separation by creating a deeper connection with our unlimited inner power. We cannot grasp a moment. It must flow into the next moment and the next moment and so on. By welcoming and trusting in the wisdom of all that has happened or is happening, we become reconciled with our past and present and we are able to let go of resistance, rejection, bitterness, anger, and hate—all of which estrange us from life and the one creative power. Believing and trusting in the wisdom of the powers of creation allows us to align ourselves with them and, thus, manifest our ideal reality. This attitude of trust and acceptance also enables our feelings of inner power as it indicates that not only do we believe in the justice and wisdom of the Universe, but also that we have faith in our own inner power and ability to deal with whatever may come. In this way, the Life Force Energy we would ordinarily lose in fearing, resisting, complaining, and rejecting what is happening becomes allocated to discovering inner powers and resources that we did not realize that we had, and probably would not have realized without these opportunities.

Often, we confuse living a life of passion with having our desires met. Living from the heart requires that we navigate the natural and instinctive aspect of desire, its essence and its forms, and the positive and the negative. It's worth contemplating while there is value in desire, there is also different degrees and flavors of desire. When we look around at Nature, we can see that for survival, all living things desire food, water, rest, and reproduction. Another aspect is human desire, also very natural and often criticized when it comes to desires that are connected to expectations, attachments, and addictions. We will never be free of having desires, but we can be free from the need to have our desires met. We do not suffer from the desires, but because we feel we need to have them met. It is possible to have many desires, but not suffer over them. Let's not discount the value of desire in that it provides contrast, and it is through contrast that makes light and growth visible where it might otherwise not be seen. On the other hand, let's not develop an addiction to desire. Let's not resign ourselves to being attached to any particular outcome.

We can use desire as a guidepost. We can allow it to steer us in new directions. It is a reminder to stay focused on what we do want and not focused on what we don't want. We can productively use desire, not becoming a slave to it, but allowing it to serve us. We are deserving of all our desires as well as abundance and growth, whether we do anything to earn them or not. Sometimes, I find myself actually enjoying the mental, physical, and emotional short-term challenges associated with desire. For example: desire for something external can bring on temporary challenges that are stimulating because they also bring out creative thinking, and this often results in accelerated transformation and feels quite empowering. So maybe it isn't that we want our life to always be filled with desires with attachments for something external, but rather that we enjoy the challenge, achievement, and transformational cycle because it is fulfilling.

There is a third aspect of desire. It is possible to be in a perpetual state of desire, similar to a perpetual state of wonder. This higher state of desire is a calling to explore all the divine gifts that the Universe has to offer us and perhaps it might feel like stepping up to the most delicious buffet of life and we get to choose whatever we want. It has no expectations or attachments—it is simply a longing in our heart to experience life fully. Perhaps the manifestation of perpetual desire is more than what is gained materially—it is about the journey towards the expression of our self, propelling us forward into life experiences that are required for a higher evolution of consciousness.

Desire comes from the mind and our Ego will not have the true answers about desire and fulfillment, but the essence of the heart does. Essence's answer does not come to us in words, but essence always answers in the present moment. It is essence that moves us forward toward a more meaningful life, filled with new experiences—ones that don't necessarily fulfill our material desires but fulfill us on much deeper levels. Essence desires all—remains open to all, expects nothing in return, and essence is where we are able to remain in a state of perpetual desire. It is the essence of feeling worthy and deserving of all that life has to offer us.

In our search for meaning in life, we begin to discover how we and other people live and think. We come to realize that answers don't just lie in economics or inequality and injustice, but to a great part in the loss of our true nature and our inability to integrate our unconscious, instinctive patterns. Looking back in time, we will see that the message of love is Universal. We all have the strength to be fully present to ourselves and others.

Passion comes from our heart and is our greatest motivator in all areas of life, relationships, work, hobbies, etc. Choose to live your life on purpose and to show up for life with great passion to joyfully create your unique life experiences and become a valuable participator in life. None of us are perfect. We forget and make mistakes. But when living from Awareness, as the observer, it is easier to re-assert your desires and witness the fruits of your intentions and transform your dreams into reality through the heart. This is bliss. This is passion!

Pay attention to what excites you. Take the time to observe and ponder yours and others in your life, your ideas, circumstances, and your values and concepts that make up your life. There is almost nothing better in the world than the feeling of showing up for our own life. When we follow our bliss or passion, life flows easily and whatever is consuming our thoughts or that enthralls us, is waiting for us to do something with it. When we show up for life, we are actively participating in being a happy person, achieving our goals, and generally living the life our soul really wants. Sometimes the passion is so great that it feels like the energy of our future self is calling us towards our inspirations and our destiny.

We cannot distance our self from life's inconsistencies, irritations, and upheavals, but we can relinquish our desire for perfect order and gain peace of mind in the process. Living a balanced life is an important part of our peace and choosing to balance not just the roles we play in life, but also the natural elements in nature's sacred spaces, is what we should be seeking. In fact, when we live from the heart, in sync with nature's rhythms, it is easier for us to ride the waves of the universal Life Force Energy, to feel more in harmony with life and the world around us.

Sometimes, the quiet lull into which we fall between ideas, projects, and goals can make life seem empty. After accomplishing one objective, you may want to move immediately on to the next. However, when your next step is unclear, you may feel frustrated, disconnected, or even suffer a mild depression. You may even perceive your lack of forward momentum as an indicator of imminent stagnation. One way to calm these distressing thoughts is to try to accept that if your intent is personal growth, you will continue to grow as an individual whether striving for a specific objective or not.

Spending time immersed in life's rigors and pleasures can be a cathartic experience that gives you the time you need to think about what you have recently gone through and leisurely contemplate what you wish to do next. You may also find that in simply being and going through the motions of everyday life, you reconnect with your priorities in a very organic, unforced way.

A mindful transitional pause can take many forms. For some, it can be a period of reflection that helps them understand how their life has unfolded. For others, it can be a period of adjustment, where new values based on recent changes are integrated into daily life. Just because we're not headed swiftly to a final destination doesn't mean we should assume that we have lost our drive. The stage between journeys can become a wonderful period of relaxation that prepares us for the path that will soon be revealed.

Feel from the heart into the blessing of being alive right now in this minute and know that every moment matters. Choosing to do more of what excites us, even if our choices require us to make certain sacrifices, fuels the feeling that our daily life is imbued with exhilaration, pleasure, and optimistic anticipation.

Sometimes we might feel a strong desire to promote what we believe in, which is definitely motivating. The more that we are passionately fervent about things that speak so strongly to our hearts, the more we notice that we can and actually do use this zeal to affect positive change in the world. Become a passionate builder and a co-creator. If whatever you're pondering makes your pulse race, makes you want to jump out of your chair and take action, soon you will find yourself riding a wave of excitement that lifts you up and makes life truly worth living.

DS: Passion has been the flame of my life and my daily fuel of energy. Passion is what makes my life magical—just like dancing or going out on a true adventure. Passion is what allows me to live life to its limits and realize that there are always opportunities for more creations, more relationships, and more love. Passion guides me to love life to its limit and lets my eternal beauty resonate with all the surroundings. What is it that makes one's mind to love life like heaven and another like hell, one body to dance with the Universe, while the other to stay still by letting the clock run out? I believe it is Awareness and understanding of the interplay between mind-heart. It is learning to shift our attention from the mind that has a tendency to create vibrations of lower energy to the heart that has higher frequencies.

We are all blessed with enormous natural capabilities and all we have to do is open up our hands, take the world into our arms, and continuously be married to life's amazement. Right at this moment you can go deeper into your heart and find all that you ever treasured and wished to do and then write down your commitments to life, imprint them into your soul, allowing them to be filled with passion. Make them your daily reminders of living.

My twelve passionate commitments to life are:

1. Embracing the precious present moment.

2. Constantly keep shifting my energy to experience the world more intimately and through Awareness.

3. Fully resonate with what surrounds me.

4. Be a reflection of eternal beauty and enjoy the mystery of time.

5. Living fully and loving well.

6. Always approach life with an attitude of happiness and a feeling of celebration.

7. Be grateful for whatever I have and have been given.

8. Flow in love and stay in love with life. This is the love that moves the sun and stars.

9. Live the reality of my own myth.

10. Use my imagination to envision my life and develop the best possibilities for my existence.

11. Have a complete willingness towards rebirth of my higher human self, my I AM.

12. Discover the harmony of life in accordance with the larger Universe and the spiritual worlds.

Our heart's desire is to love and live life as a true celebration. Passion is what places our soul on fire and keeps the flame burning in our heart. Passion lives within every one of our body cells and reveals itself as freedom, excitement, energy, and enthusiasm.

Live in a world of celebration. The magic of living and loving is found in your own garden of love and your own temple of light. Let all pleasures of life be guided by the divine Eros of Agape. Be a passionate spirit of creation. Each moment is a precious gift and you are the master artist of your own life. Open up your heart and eyes to the world—count your blessings. Life is delicious and glorious. Your love will melt all kinds of boundaries and allow you to light up the world with your bliss.

Going Deeper

CR: Our lives are made up of a complex network of pathways that we can use to move from one phase of life to the next. For some of us, our paths are wide, smooth, and clearly marked. Many people, however, find that they have a difficult time figuring out where they need to go next. Determining which "next step" will land you on the most direct route to happiness, fulfillment, and the realization of your life purpose may not seem easy.

There are many ways to discover what the next step on your life path should be. If you are someone who seeks to satisfy your soul, it is vital that you make this inquiry. Often, your inner voice will counsel you that it's time for a change, and it is very important to trust yourself because only you know what is best for you. To live from the heart, you have to ask some powerful questions. These include:

What am I taking for granted?

How can I show my appreciation for others?

What can I do to take care of those I love?

How can I be more present?

Who am I blaming or mad at?

Who do I need to forgive?

Where can I be more accountable and what am I responsible for?

What am I thankful for?

How can I take better care of myself?

What action do I need to take to make sure I have no regrets?

Journaling

CR: For this journal entry write in detail about the life you would like to live. People who get what they want tend to be the ones who make the effort to know what they want. If we feel confined in a tiny limited life, imagine the life you would like to be living.

Ways to discover the limits of the life we want is to listen to our heart and use our imagination. Once you have written down your best life story, it is time to visualize your life, making sure to place yourself in the vision. From the place of Awareness, become the observer of yourself as you walk around in your vision. Notice what you are doing in your vision and from the heart, not the mind. Notice how it feels to you. Now venture a little way past the vision into the energy of outrageous awesome possibilities. Relax in this space, asking the following questions:

Is my vision the highest and best use of my life?

Will this give me energy or deplete my energy?

How do I define success?

What am I grateful for?

What are my blind spots?

What am I pretending not to know?

What good is there that I presently cannot see?

How can I become the space for attracting this vision of my life?

Stay loose and relaxed as you're conjuring up the various possibilities and be sure to take them all through the heart. You'll notice that some of them leave you with a feeling of intrigue, curiosity, and a bit lighter. These are your preferences. Now let them tiptoe into your consciousness. Simply allow them, watching them as an observer, to let the vision take form, leaving a vague impression, and then go for a bit more specificity as if you were bringing a camera into zoom focus. Allow and watch.

If you remain playful and patient, the preferences forming in your consciousness will eventually become clear enough to describe the preference in more detail in your journal. Still wait—don't jump the gun. Hold on a bit longer and you will observe what I call maximum specificity by pinpointing the desires. Let them simply unfold.

Stay with the vision. Take it to your heart and ask yourself, "What would be even better?" After allowing another answer to come into focus, ask yourself, "What would be even better than that?" Repeat this process until you have an image of a life that is so perfect, you can't imagine any way to top it. This is pinpoint clarity. Once you have pinpoint clarity, practice visualizing your dream daily. I have found it is best to do this exercise first thing in the morning or last thing at night.

Connect with Others

CR: Sometimes we tend to protect our seeds of dreams, desires, and passions by wrapping them in the business of our daily ambitions and grandiose plans that have nothing at all to do with the sweetness and ripeness that already exists within us. Remember the story of the peach in an earlier chapter; none of our plans and goals can prepare us for the moment we ripen. What we can do is try not to define ourselves by all the layers covering us. When we are ripe within, our soul fills out like a mature fruit, and once ripened, we are able to feel compassion and joy underneath the soft fuzzy covering of the stories we got used to telling ourselves. Nothing matters but the sweetness within the heart.

Start a conversation with a friend or loved one sharing the experience and your insights from your journaling. Realize what is real for you and open a discussion of the current state of your being with regards to living life from your heart. Discuss the current state of your life and how you feel about it. Reflect on how many goals and dreams you have incubated and all the hours you have spent weaving your dreams into stories you tell yourself, some that never came to the fruition you hoped for. Sometimes we work for years covering our own wounds of esteem and the ups and downs of our accomplishments until our heart is covered over with only our perceived achievements. It is only when we lay aside our achievements that the light from our heart begins to take on a new form. The light will never force itself into our hearts. It is very patient and seems to wait for us to open enough so the light can enter—filling whatever space we have been able to empty out within our self.

Milestones

CR: While celebrations are sometimes intended to honor life's more momentous occasions, much of real life tends to happen during the in-between times. While moving from one moment in time to the next is seldom considered a significant occurrence, it is during those in-between times that we are most in tune with life's most profound, albeit simple joys. Celebrating the in-between times can be as easy as paying special attention to them when they do happen, rather than taking them for granted.

The beauty of Life is happening all around us and to us between the pauses that we take to honor our journey through life. It's our focus of attention that can turn an in-between time into a celebration. Pay homage to each moment by slowing down and allowing yourself time to look around at the beauty of nature, by opening our hearts and minds to take in all of life's wonders. Far too often, we let those simple moments of awe pass us by. Celebrate this major milestone to begin to live a life of passion from the heart.

The Mind is the Map

It is time to return to balance—a balance of equanimity—
a balance that celebrates diversity among cultures, races
and religions—a balance with nature and our
ecosystems—a balance of justice and freedom for all.
We need the power of the mind and the warmth of
the heart to learn to live in a world that is constantly
changing. Today, more than ever, we have the capabilities
to co-create our lives with the rest of the world and
the Universe.

FINDING JOY

XII

Creating
Our
New Story

PART II:

CULTIVATING THE JOURNEY

"The ultimate measure of a person is not where he or she stands in moments of comfort and convenience, but where he or she stands at times of challenge and controversy."

- Martin Luther King, Jr.

CHAPTER TWELVE

CREATING OUR NEW STORY

C R: EVERYTHING IS changing. There is an awakening happening now and people are changing the way they view their lives and the world around them. Many have reached the limit of what we can see only with the rational mind, fully understanding that we cannot comprehend everything that happens in our magnificent and beautiful world and perhaps we need to take a broader higher-level view.

The current world events seem to be changing in the blink of an eye, stirring things up, and a lot of the information and misinformation is sending conflicting energy out into the collective consciousness of humanity along with a host of predictions, possibilities, and probable outcomes. A good deal of this energy is fear based. This is a time to let our voices be heard. It is a time for our voices to make their way to the light. We need to work on removing our habitual human hesitation that keeps us from our own unique expression. We need to feel what is rising within us. We need to express what it is we are feeling and this can be done from the heart in a soft and gentle way.

Using Emotional Intelligence is one way to navigate through all this global information, to know our own depth, and to wait for our own associations and reflex reactions to subside and settle. This helps us to not project negative energy onto each other or out into the collective energetic footprint of all humanity. It is in our stillness we are able to become transparent enough to see ourselves and each other clearly.

Like the blinking of our eyes, the world around us blinks in and out of darkness thousands of times each day and seems to be a reflex, one that we often have no control over. However, what we do have control over is how we choose to react. As human beings, our hearts and minds also blink, opening and closing thousands of times a day. A question we might ask ourselves is, "Do we see darkness with intermittent streams of light? Or do we see light with intermittent streams of darkness?" Perhaps there will never be an answer to this question. But if we ponder on it often throughout our day, we may find, through personal alchemy, that we are able to feel hope instead of despair, feel optimism instead of pessimism, and be at peace knowing that all is well instead of living with the fear of the unknown. Perhaps wisdom can be found in between the blinking. We all need to stand up for our true self and to take the time to stand before each other as we risk expressing our truth. We need to be able to hold a loving space and become active listeners for others allowing them to break through with their wisdom and truth.

Companies are employing Emotional Intelligence in their executive management teams and this action is beginning to change corporate cultures, because they have no choice. People are using their money as a tool for change in support of consciousness in the marketplace. I see so much information related to these issues. People are raising their voices and sharing in consciousness with others. Perhaps the old business and employment model isn't working anymore. More and more people are reaching their limit of working in big corporations that are not conscious corporations. Many suffer stress and anxiety working under these conditions.

A feeling of wanting to make a difference in our lives and the world we live in is reaching new peaks and the lack of purpose is seemingly knocking at the door of many by way of messages from the heart. Savvy entrepreneurs with brilliant ideas and passions are offering new models of entrepreneurship and assigning new attributes for leadership with the focus on what are the requirements for dynamic leaders in today's fast paced and ever-changing world. Many are creating new business models offering solutions aligned with consciousness and right actions, including environmental concerns that are now emerging on a global scale. We are finally beginning to understand what consciousness in the business world might look like and many are building and operating such organizations.

The Internet has proved to be an incredibly powerful tool for connecting people who are consciously aligned and after many years, we are beginning to understand this enormous power. The world has opened up, as the separation ends, barriers collapse, unity is the new movement. The practice of Emotional Intelligence is the new action that is exploding as people join together in a synergistic manner. Co-operation and co-creating on a global scale are happening. There is a rise in kindness, compassion, empathy, sharing, helping, giving hands, and getting united. Right thought and right action are leading the way supporting collaborative global unity. All these new movements are indicative of, and inclusive of, the use and practice of Emotional Intelligence.

We are seeing this change all around the world. The small farmer is starting to have strength again. People are buying locally and from food sources they trust and many others are planting their own food, and that changes the whole economy. Mass farming operations owned by large corporations are not trusted nor are the organizations that are not willing to inform us what it is we are eating.

There is a drastic fall in over-the-top consumer consumption. For many years, we have been manipulated, stimulated to consume more and more; to purchase everything new that is launched in the market. To have the newest car, the latest iPhone, the best brands, lots of clothes, lots of shoes, lots of lots, lots of everything. Now many people are changing their buying habits. They understand that it makes no sense at all and how destructive this consumption is to our ecosystem.

Emotional Intelligence is fostering a new consciousness of moving more towards a slow life and slow food, zero personal debt, and this change is beginning to show us that in the past we have organized ourselves in the most absurd way possible and a way that is not sustainable for humanity and our planet. Every time more people trade clothes, donate, buy old things, share goods, share cars, apartments, offices—we contribute to this new movement of higher consciousness. We truly need nothing of what we have been conditioned by media and advertising as to what we need. This conscious action can and will break any corporation that depends on exaggerated consumption.

We are beginning to see changes in our education systems, with the realization that the current model of teaching to test no longer works. This is an old outdated teaching model that conditions our children to be followers of a dysfunctional system and prepares them to become ordinary citizens that conform to a society of beliefs that no longer works. Fortunately, there are many people working to change that.

Movements all over the world are seeing and changing the current model to ones more fitting and more aligned with the needs of today and the vision of conscious societies. Cultivating Awareness, and the practice of Emotional Intelligence, invite collaboration, co-operation and co-creating in groups, problem solving and addressing issues that require change for a more sustainable future for humanity and for our world itself and will continue to make a difference.

Throughout history, this wrestling with strength and power has been characterized in all cultures, which represent the best and worst of what it means to be human. Both of these energies live within each of us and we are able to respond instantaneously to whatever challenge we are faced with using Emotional Intelligence. When we are living in pure Awareness and from our center, a connective embodied power arises that unifies all life and such embodiments can be heroic in the deepest sense. When we face our challenges head on and from our center, we discover and are able to take a stand in our place in the Universe. Facing our potential, we are called to enter a journey of discovery and not surprisingly living from the heart, which is our center of Source and Oneness that gives us the strength to manifest the highest possible outcome in the many varied experiences we find ourselves in.

There is duality in this potential, as there is in all things, and we are called to face the dragon or unleashed power of others, while standing up to old systems that are no longer working and people who are not living from their center. Some have become disruptive agents that dishearten all they touch. We are charged to stand in our center in order to not be overtaken by this energy. Perhaps it is a function of the Universe to balance that causes us to face these sometimes troubling and confusing experiences.

On a deeper level, perhaps facing our potential is the call to summon our best qualities in order to face someone, something, some force that is challenging. And perhaps this one thing, one force, or someone, is not always bad or dangerous. It is simply that life often demands that we face things in order to transform them—a process we often miss or tend to resist. It is persistence and facing our challenges that can transform us into our truest self. To "face" does not mean to resist or to defeat, but to encounter honestly. And to "be" does not mean to retreat from this world, but to merge with it from a centered place of strength.

Martin Luther King Jr. revealed an inextricable link between power and love when he said, *"Power when properly understood is nothing but the ability to achieve purpose. And one of the great problems of history is that the concepts of love and power have usually been contrasted as opposites... polar opposites... so that love is identified with a resignation of power, and power with a denial of love. We've got to get this thing right. What is needed is a realization that power without love is reckless and abusive, and love without power is sentimental and anemic. Power at its best is love implementing the demands of justice, and justice at its best is power correcting everything that stands against love. It is precisely this collision of immoral power with powerless morality which constitutes the major crisis of our time."*

It seems like this question has always been asked. That is, "How do we define these elements?" Is strength the art of authority, of achieving domination over situations and others, as rulers throughout history have shown us? Or is strength of the art of embrace, of surrendering to the power of love and truth rising up within us? We all carry the seed of each element—the power of authority and the power of embrace. May we all use our power for our optimal potential to live as illuminated beings.

Conditions aren't always perfect and waiting for the perfection of "someday" might just mean that will take our dreams with us when we depart this earthly plane. Nothing in life is good or bad and if our dream is important to us, and we're thinking to do it somewhere down the road, why not just do it now in the present moment—the only moment that exists.

Sometimes in the beginning all we need is to make minor changes to our life's blueprint and make corrections along the way. The point is to just start to make things happen. As we gain momentum, we'll begin to experience bigger and better changes and growth in our lives and as a result, growth in our happiness too.

It is a time to return to balance—a balance of equanimity—a balance that celebrates diversity among cultures, races and religions—a balance with nature and our eco systems—a balance of justice and freedom for all, and a balance of the masculine and feminine energies. This balance begins with each one of us and we can make a difference. It's not easy, but we can do it. Until we have peace in our own individual lives, we will not have peace in our outer world.

Many of us are currently experiencing circumstances that require us to restore harmony and balance in our lives and cultivate peace within ourselves and within our closest relationships. Once we do this, we are better able to extend this balance and peace outward to personal, social, economic and governmental relationships, untangling and unwinding all existing human programs, structures, and processes and create a new story for Humanity—one that serves all people in light and love.

We can expect that many old systems may collapse in a domino-like effect from this revolutionary pressure to create change. There is a new foundational platform emerging and as we embrace this awakening and the changes, we are seeing the highest and most positive potential of humanity approaching. Wherever we are in our personal journey, and no matter where we are on this planet, we are all feeling the shift deep within that is our calling to a cosmic awakening. This is an extremely exciting and inspiring time for most of us as we are experiencing and witnessing a critical change in our collective consciousness. The unconditionally loving and kind hearted are the most powerful alchemists spiriting this awakening.

DS: Our heart is more than our body's most important organ—it's also the essence of our spiritual and emotional being. Listening to our heart is much more valuable than always making decisions with just your head.

"Is our mind an instrument of the heart or its master?"

HEART'S DIALOGUE WITH BRAIN

"The heart is actually the inner organ of perception, by means of which the head perceives everything that takes place in the body. The heart is the center of the Universe."

- Rudolf Steiner

"Follow Your Heart ...our hearts may actually be the 'intelligent force' behind the intuitive thoughts and feelings we all experience."

- Joseph Chilton Pearce

We are highly sophisticated beings. However, we have taught ourselves to rely on the mind's intellect and forget to synchronize with our heart. Our thinking process, and not our thoughts, is a spiritual gift from God and while we have placed great intelligence within the bounds of the mind, it is our heart that connects us to Universal intelligence and our Life Force Energy. Our entire world lives in our heart and along with our true essence, creates our most fulfillment. Our heart offers beauty and warmth and maintains all relationships between and within our cells, organs, brain, body, and the world. And our heart is the center of all feelings—our joyful and loving compass of life and the center of our spiritual existence in this world.

A few years ago, while attending a seminar, I met a great author and human being. His name was Joseph Chilton Pearce. For more than a century, Joseph has been probing the mysteries of the human mind and has written many successful books on the relationship between heart and mind. Joseph has demonstrated that beneath our Awareness, our culture imprints a negative force field that blocks the natural rise of our soul and spirit.

We need to be aware of how the collective unconscious and social environment has and continues to shape our life.

What influential social models, patterns, and factors are shaping our lives?

How are our religious beliefs affecting our thinking?

What is more important that our social environment?

What limits our growth?

We are all part of a new awakening, something larger than ourselves. Our own revelation and discovery of our own true and perfect nature can only come from heart awareness and a healthy balance with our mind.

Great philosophers like Aristotle, Rudolf Steiner, and others have provided similar information on the roles of heart and mind. Rudolf Steiner explains that our heart instant by instant registers and reflects back the ongoing events of the world and that all of our feelings develop in the heart, not the mind. According to Aristotle, compared to other living beings, the warmth of the heart is the most purely formed and developed. Indeed, our heart does not rely on intellectual thoughts and has an inherent capacity of warmth for movement, life processes, and soul development.

Your heart is the center of your being and your spiritual existence in the world.

Let us take charge of our thoughts and allow them to flow through the golden light of our heart. The mind is an instrument of our heart and its servant. Let us keep shifting our thoughts into the heart and allow its warmth to offer beauty, unconditional love, and many other capabilities. Our heart is the true Queen, the center of our delightful feelings, and the secret fire of our soul. Our mind's peace is in the heart and when the mind and heart are working in balanced unison, we can remain open to life's wonder.

We need the power of the mind and the warmth of the heart to learn to live in a world that is constantly changing. New technology, new choices, and new areas are there to explore. We have collected incredible amounts of data and have great knowledge about our Earth, our planets, and the Universe. Today, more than ever, we have the capabilities to co-create harmonious lives with the rest of the world and the Universe.

At the same time, we need to learn how to question this new information and technology and learn how to avoid the magnetism of the news and social media that attempt to influence our lives. There is no doubt the new information has improved our life, health, business, farming, and overall environment. We now have the ability to communicate on a global scale and share new ideas of what is working and what is not. While all this new information has brought a positive change to our life, the artificial technology and extensive Internet use has resulted in much exterior absorbing at the cost of developing our own mind. We have become pre-occupied with what's going on "out there." Furthermore, the social media and constant promotion of negative news, and "nonsense news" attempts to distort our perception of reality, magnify our fears and doubts, and creates great tension in our lives.

If we decide to take a journey into the past, we will find periods of times when people lived in a true state of consciousness, peace, and Eudaimonia. Our ancestors experienced the wisdom of "know thyself" inscribed in the holy temple of Apollo in Delphi. Knowing thyself meant self-awareness and connection to the higher self.

While we are living with the new age of technology and the social world, we need to remain strong in our roots and bring into consciousness the collective unconscious that keeps us hostages. By becoming Alchemists of the heart, we can purify our soul and transform all the mind debris collected over the years.

During our new journey of meaning and purpose, we learn from courageous people who have shaped our world and whose acts, strength, and goodness has served our society well. People like Gandhi, Martin Luther King, Helen Keller, Rosa Parks, Mother Teresa, Nelson Mandela, and Princess Diana have taught us the value of the heart. Their courage and awareness have given us the freedom over conformity to social standards and collective thought.

The key to the story of my own life has been my ability to maintain fluidity and flexibility. Awareness and courage allowed me to differentiate between winning and losing, quitting or moving ahead, standing up or picking up the next battle. I have come to a self-realization that no matter what the Universe sends, it has to be accepted as a gift and a loan from God. This means, keep embracing all kinds of events and keep revealing life's magic knowing that each time you face opposition you are getting closer to your destiny.

Destiny is not something we create, but something that we work on. You become consistent to processes, such as embracing the precious present moment, being aware of habitual patterns and old beliefs, and living within the tapestry of life.

Let us remain open to the idea that, although we live in an unpredictable world, each day there are new meaningful coincidences and situations and each and every one of these will shape our life and create our new empowering story.

*"If the doors of perception were cleansed
everything would appear to man as it is, Infinite.
For man has closed himself up, till he sees all
things thro' narrow chinks of his cavern."*

- William Blake,
The Marriage of Heaven and Hell

EPILOGUE

THE IDEAS AND processes put forward in this book, *The Mind is The Map,* are simply a pathway to understand our self and why we do what we do. They provide a way to transform the old ways of thinking from the mind, moving to new ways of thinking from the heart. We are learning that everything we have ever been programmed into believing was our reality is being shaken down to the core. As we learn to think and act from our hearts, we will continue to break free from the controlled minds of the individual and the programming of the conditioned masses. This is a time for cooperation and for embracing transformational processes that will help ease us though this change. The more we commit to knowing ourselves, knowing our soul, at a heart level, the easier this transformation becomes.

No matter what our exterior experiences look like in the present moment, we can create new realities by choosing new thoughts moment by moment. We have infinite possibilities to live from our hearts as we continue to grow stronger and as more of us remember to live our divine purpose and love for the sake of love. The choice to live in our personal power lies with every individual.

We cannot run away from emotional vulnerability or hide from each other any longer. The level of inner balance and spiritual and emotional maturity that we are able to accept will reflect in our relationships, our inner self and the "spiritual assignment" we call our life purpose. We are ending the ways in which we casually live and view our world and all of our interactions with others will be first and foremost about personal transformation and spiritual development.

A new foundational template will emphasize this change in human relationships on a global scale. We are being asked to move away from destructive archetypes that resist and delude the perception between us and them. It is a time for a deep reflection in our understanding of the nature of the history of humanity. It is a time to take a great leap and rewrite a new story for our future. It is a time to realize that all relationships with our fellow man have been about spiritual growth through applied life lessons. Now it is time to participate with that comprehension in order to easily graduate to the next level of what it will be like to be human and live from the heart as unconditional love.

Benevolence is everywhere if we accept the responsibility. However, it requires each of us to go within and trust our Spirit, surrendering to our higher power with no exceptions or conditions. We do this by bringing our minds, hearts and souls into alignment. This journey is not easy and it requires many small steps, as well as patience and courage through the process. It is our hope that as you moved through these pages and integrated the processes outlined in this book, that your hearts open wider than they may have ever done before, allowing you more clarity about your purpose in life, helping you become more inspired about this magnificent Universe we live in and to enable your human mind to awaken to its divine birthright.

Whatever path lay before us on our journey—whatever puzzles we must take apart and put back together—the secret of life has to do with the awakening and freeing of what has been unseen and asleep. It is so for the history of all of humanity and it is the humbling story of accepting our own unique life as it is revealed. It is a collective story of humanity, an individual story, and one that requires our full attention. It is one of sweet compassion; a never-ending story of how we embrace each other, and forgive ourselves, as we find our place in the Oneness of all that is. No amount of thinking can eliminate the wonder and the pain of living. With whatever difficulty that arises or crisis we experience, there is a voice that speaks beneath our pain and if we can slow down enough to hear it and believe it, it will guide us and lead us to our heart space where the inescapable act of transformation begins. It is both beautiful and difficult to realize who we really are, and that we are part of everything. This is the love that moves us into Oneness.

May we all continue to embrace attitudes of hope, faith, cooperation, compassion and equanimity. May we all take right action from our loving hearts and may we all practice unconditional love and forgiveness. Through our balanced self-mastery, we as individuals and as a collective society have the ability to create the most loving, peaceful, and spiritual new world ever imagined.

Love and Blessings…Christina and Dimitrios

CHRISTINA REEVES

Born in Toronto, Canada, Christina is a Holistic Life Coach and

Energy Psychologist. She is also an accomplished author, speaker, and facilitator, hosting workshops, seminars and lectures in North America and internationally. Following a successful career as an entrepreneur, mentor and coach, she made a conscious choice to shift her focus to one she was passionate about and one with a stronger bottom line than simply commerce for commerce sake. Over the past fifteen years she has developed her own programs for assisting others in the process of self-discovery and personal transformation. The Writing on Our Walls is one such program. Working from her clinic and training facility she continues to share her methodologies and techniques mentoring and supporting others to take responsibility in reaching their full potential while guiding them towards enjoying a joyful and happy life.